Watering Systems
for
Lawn & Garden

Watering Systems
for
Lawn & Garden

A Do-It-Yourself Guide

R. Dodge Woodson

A Storey Publishing Book

Storey Communications, Inc.
Schoolhouse Road
Pownal, Vermont 05261

*The mission of Storey Communications is to serve our customers
by publishing practical information that encourages personal independence
in harmony with the environment.*

Edited by Deborah L. Balmuth
Cover design by Greg Imhoff and Cynthia McFarland
Cover photographs by Nicholas Whitman
Text design and production by Cynthia McFarland
Production assistance by Susan Bernier
Line drawings by Raymond Wood, wash drawings by Brigita Fuhrmann, combined and
    modified by Cynthia McFarland
Technical review by Emilio Cardinali and John Kemp
Indexed by Northwind Editorial Services

Copyright © 1996 by R. Dodge Woodson

The information in this book is true and complete to the best of our knowledge. All recommendations are made
without guarantee on the part of the author or Storey Communications, Inc. The author and publisher disclaim
any liability in connection with the use of this information. For additional information please contact Storey
Communications, Inc., Schoolhouse Road, Pownal, Vermont 05261.

Printed in the United States by Vicks Lithograph & Printing Corporation

10 9 8 7 6 5 4 3 2

Library of Congress Cataloging-in-Publication Data

Woodson, R. Dodge (Roger Dodge), 1955-
    Watering systems for lawn and garden : a do-it-yourself guide / R. Dodge Woodson.
                p.   cm.
    "A Storey Publishing book."
    Includes index.
    ISBN 0-88266-906-0 (pbk. : alk. paper)
    1. Lawns—Irrigation—Equipment and supplies—Handbooks, manuals, etc. 2. Gar-
dens—Irrigation—Equipment and supplies—Handbooks, manuals, etc. 3. Sprinklers—Handbooks,
manuals, etc. 4. Sprinkler irrigation—Equipment and supplies—Handbooks, manuals, etc. 5. Irrigation—Equipment and supplies—Handbooks, manuals, etc. I. Title.
        SB433.2.W66 1996
        635'.0487—dc20   95-30587
                                                                              CIP

Contents

Introduction

IF YOU'RE THINKING OF BUYING or installing an irrigation system for your lawn or backyard garden, this book was written for you. Regardless of whether you're interested in a high-tech, automatic sprinkler system or simple, mobile irrigation equipment, you'll find answers to your questions.

Lawns and small gardens can be watered in a variety of ways. Sometimes all that is needed is a sprinkler and garden hose. Other jobs call for more sophisticated equipment, such as an overhead irrigation system, underground irrigation system, or a more complex surface system. Each type has its place and its advantages. This book will show them all.

The quantity of water used in irrigation can be staggering. It can, in fact, be of such demand on a well that the well is rendered useless for a while. If a well supplies your water, think twice before using it for your lawn or garden. Extended dry spells put enough of a burden on some wells that the added responsibility as a source of irrigation is just too much for the well to handle. There are ways, however, to avoid this problem, which you will learn as you read through this book.

Reading technical material about irrigation can be a bit on the dry side, but you won't find that to be the case here. Yes, you will get plenty of technical information, but you won't get it in a boring, textbook style.

If you've ever read instructions for putting together a bicycle or for programming a VCR, you have some idea of how difficult it can be to understand highly technical terms. I have presented these technical instructions in clear, easy-to-understand language, with step-by-step directions leaving nothing to the imagination. You won't need to read a paragraph three or four times to understand what I'm saying.

Can you install your own irrigation system? There is little doubt that you *can* — almost anyone can with the help of this book. Assuming that you *need* an irrigation system, installing it yourself can save you a lot of money, plus you will gain a sense of self-satisfaction beyond financial gain.

Will this book tell you everything there is to know about irrigation? No, but it will give you all the information you need to buy or build and install your own irrigation system. All the equipment and applications covered in this book are directed at the homeowner's needs, which are different from those of commercial farmers and golf course owners. This book is written specifically for residential and small-scale gardening irrigation.

My own experience — both personal and professional — has led me to write this book. I've lived in the country most of my life. As a child, my grandparents took care of me while my parents worked. My father has always been proud of maintaining a pretty lawn, but he was never into gardening. My grandfather enjoyed vegetable gardening and growing experimental (grafted) fruit trees. A rose garden — and I mean a big one — was my grandmother's passion. During those early years, I received quite an extensive education in gardening and lawn care.

Back in those days, I gave each tomato plant a fresh drink of tap water with a watering can. I planted seeds, pulled weeds, helped run the rototiller, and kept Japanese beetles off the roses. During unusually hot spells, I spent most of my time toting water between the two gardens and running through the sprinkler.

This was the beginning of my water career, as I later became a plumber.

As a teenager, I kept a small garden of my own, which was a source of pride for me. I enjoyed working in it until hunting, fishing, girls, and four-wheel-drive trucks became more important. During my adventuresome years, I took a sabbatical from gardening.

After completing construction of my first home in the heat of a Virginia summer, I returned to gardening. It was then that I discovered how quickly a shallow well can run dry. The grass seed didn't have much chance to penetrate the hard-baked ground, and as a result, I brought out the water hoses and sprinklers. Unfortunately, it didn't take long for my new well to start spitting sand. The water reserve simply wasn't adequate. I had no grass that year.

Much has changed since the days of my grandparents' gardens, when I helped even before I could read the words on seed packages and learned the value of a good watering plan. I've continued to expand my knowledge over the years, and some thirty years later, I'm still learning. It seems that every year I find a way to make gardening easier. As a busy plumber and businessman, husband and father, I've looked for shortcuts, and the ones I've found I would like to share with you in this book.

You will get detailed, hands-on advice. The goal is to concentrate on specific issues in each chapter and suggest methods that may best suit your small-scale irrigation needs. I also introduce some products that you may not know exist. My goal is for you to have fun and learn at the same time. To get started, let's talk about some of the obstacles you may encounter around your own home.

When a Watering Can Won't Work: Preliminary Considerations

I F YOU ENJOY A GREEN LAWN AND lush garden, you may have discovered already that there are times when a watering can just won't work. We all know that grass, flowers, and vegetables need water to thrive, but what can we do when needed water won't fall from the sky? Most of us pull out the garden hose, and perhaps a cheap sprinkler, to meet our plants' need for water. Sometimes this works fine, but sometimes it doesn't.

Common Watering Problems

If you have a large lawn or garden, you may have found that a garden hose is not practical as your only irrigation device. Not only can you spend a lot of time watering, you can also waste a lot of water.

Water Is Scarce or Expensive

During hot, dry spells, shallow wells tend to use up water reserves quickly. If you're not careful, in addition to having parched lawns and gardens, you also may have no household water for drinking, cooking, or bathing, which is serious.

People with shallow wells are not the only ones who want an efficient way to water their greenery. Municipal water supplies provide nearly endless reserves of water to many homeowners, but the cost of this service can add up considerably when watering a lawn or garden.

The Can Gets Heavier

If you use a watering can for your garden, you may have noticed that the can gets heavier with each passing summer. (I know *I* found this to be true.) Watering cans are fine for around the home and for tiny flower gardens, but once your watering needs grow, so must your method of irrigation. There are many ways to eliminate the need for a watering can, but some of these options are plagued with problems.

The Hose Is Too Short

How many times have you laid out a garden hose only to find that it just doesn't quite reach the area that needs water? Have you ever left your hose filled with pressure only to come back and find that it has swollen and split? Do you resent having to roll up the hose frequently to keep from killing the grass trying to grow under it? Isn't it amazing what can happen when you run over a garden hose with a lawn mower? And how about those kinks in the hose that cut off the water just as you are ready to get started? These problems, and many more like them, can make working with a garden hose more trouble than it is worth.

The Yard Is Too Big

A common complaint by the time an August sun has burned the grass to a crisp is that the yard is too big to water effectively. This is a legitimate complaint. Without some type of automatic watering system, large lawns can shrivel up and die. Trying to water a few acres of lawn with water hoses and sprinklers can be nearly a full-time job.

Never at Home Long Enough

One of the most common complaints of homeowners with scorched grass is that they never are home long enough to maintain a regular watering schedule. This is a "routine" problem; one that an automatic sprinkling system can solve quickly. The biggest problem you will have in solving your not-enough-time dilemma will be choosing a system that suits your budget as well as your need.

Watering Options

Once you've decided to go beyond the watering can and garden hose, you'll want to explore the options. The type of watering system that will work best for you depends on your needs, resources, and your personal task.

Overhead Irrigation Systems

Overhead irrigation systems usually are not practical for lawns, but they work well for gardens. Since an overhead system remains set up throughout the irrigation season, it must be sturdy and dependable.

Installing an overhead irrigation system can range from simple to complex. The system may amount to little more than a few posts, some tomato stakes or lattice, and some piping. While this type of system may not make the cover of a magazine for its aesthetics, it is a cost-effective and practical way to solve your watering problems.

If appearance is important to you, however, an overhead irrigation system need not be ruled out, since there are many ways to make it attractive. For instance, building a framework around your garden can create the image of a small park. You can install an arched doorway, a trellis, some latticework, and other decorative trim to conceal your irrigation system. This not only works, it looks good.

Overhead systems are easy to install. There is minimum trenching to be done, and most of the work is exposed and accessible. Also, materials can be inexpensive. Polybutylene pipe, for instance, is an excel-lent irrigation material and costs a fraction of the price for copper tubing. We'll get into more detail on design and costs of overhead systems later in Chapter 7.

Underground Irrigation Systems

Underground irrigation systems are ideal for lawns. Pop-up sprinkler heads and automatic timers make these systems one of the best available for keeping a yard

Overhead Irrigation Systems Are:

~ Not practical for most lawn applications

~ Ideal for both flower and vegetable gardens

~ Simple to install

~ Inexpensive to install

~ Not always attractive, but can be made to be

~ Able to be installed without trenching

~ Not excessive in the amount of water required for operation

~ A simulation of natural rainfall

~ Able to be taken down after the irrigation season

~ Suitable for almost any size garden

Underground Irrigation Systems Are:

~ Practical for lawn applications

~ Suitable, in most cases, for both flower and vegetable gardens

~ Not extremely difficult to install

~ Likely to be expensive to install

~ Attractive and unobtrusive

~ Convenient to use after initial installation

~ Often in need of high water pressure and volume

~ Able to be programmed with a timer to activate automatically

~ Subject to freezing in cold climates and require winteri-zation in such locations

~ Suitable for lawns and gardens of all sizes

WHEN A WATERING CAN WON'T WORK

moist and lush. Cost can be a drawback, however, because these systems are not cheap. You won't have to mortgage your home to pay for one, but you may have to catch your breath for a moment before writing the check.

Due to the plowing and tilling that takes place in a garden, using an underground system is rarely practical. However, since there are rows of undisturbed ground in and around a flower garden, an underground system can be an excellent source of irrigation for this type of garden. Installing an underground system involves trenching though, so if you cringe at the thought of digging up your beautiful ground, you may want to investigate other types of systems.

Mobile Irrigation Equipment

Mobile irrigation equipment can be the least expensive option for watering lawns and gardens. In this context, we are not talking about the large, long-range sprinklers used with firehoses by commercial farmers. We are talking about standard garden hoses

Mobile Irrigation Systems Are:

~ Practical for lawn applications

~ Suitable for both flower and vegetable gardens

~ Mobile, so no installation is required

~ An inexpensive irrigation option

~ Not left in place constantly, so appearance isn't a major factor

~ Compatible with the water pressure serving most homes

~ Inconvenient to use, since they must be set up and moved periodically

~ Suitable for lawns and gardens of all sizes

Drip Irrigation Systems Are:

~ Not practical for lawn applications

~ Suitable for both flower and vegetable gardens

~ Fairly simple to install

~ Affordable

~ Unobtrusive

~ Compatible with the water pressure serving most homes

~ Convenient to use

~ Suitable for gardens of all sizes

~ An ideal way to water the root zone of individual plants

~ Not conducive to erosion

and consumer-grade sprinklers. For small plots of ground, this system can be very effective.

One problem with mobile irrigation equipment is the need to move and reconstruct it periodically, which takes time. For "time-conscious people," a more permanent system is desirable.

Drip Systems

Drip systems can be as simple as overhead piping with tiny holes that allow water to drip out at a steady rate. More sophisticated drip systems utilize special components to control the exact flow of water. The use of drip systems in flower and vegetable gardens can be very effective. The drip locations can be pinpointed near the root zone of individual plants. Since water drips out slowly and finds its target easily, less water is used to maintain constant irrigation, which is a big advantage over a sprinkler system.

While drip systems are not practical for watering lawns, they are an ideal choice for targeted watering of specific plants, shrubs, and trees.

Water Sources

When most people think of watering lawns and gardens, they think of screwing a water hose onto an outside faucet, which, of course, is usually the most convenient method. It also is one of the most obvious sources of water, but not the only or best means of irrigation. There are many sources for water. Let's take a brief look at some of them.

City Water

If your home is served by city water, you may not need any other water source. As long as there is no moratorium on watering and you can afford the water bill, you are pretty much set. Tapping into the pipes that serve your home with potable (drinking) water will not be much of a chore, and you will have a nearly endless supply of water.

Dug Wells

Dug wells often run dry in hot, summer months. Of course, some wells do better than others. If your house is served by a dug well, you should be able to do some light irrigation without cutting off the water supply to your home, but don't plan on extensive watering unless your well has an unusually high recovery rate (the period of time it takes for a well to replenish its water supply). For example, a well with a recovery rate of 5 gallons per minute (gpm) will produce 5 gallons of water every minute until it has reached its balance point. As water is pumped out, the well will continue to replace the water at this recovery rate.

Drilled Wells

Drilled wells are expensive, but offer vast amounts of water, since they are drilled deep into the earth. A 300-foot well is not uncommon in Maine, and wells with depths of 100 and 200 feet are normal in many places. Since drilled wells are so deep, they often hit aquifers with fast flow rates. While a typical drilled well produces at least 5 gallons of water per minute, some have recovery rates in excess of

20 gpm, and that's a lot of water. A drilled well is probably your best bet, if you have to irrigate an expansive area in a rural setting.

Driven-Point Wells

Driven-point wells are the least expensive to fashion. They are made by driving sections of pipe into the ground, one section at a time, until water is hit, at which point a pump is added and you have water. Any handy homeowner can make a driven-point well.

We're going to talk more about different types of wells and other water sources in the chapters that follow, so don't worry about getting the whole picture right now. You are learning about options for irrigation, and as we progress you will learn the nitty-gritty about these subjects.

Streams and Ponds

Streams and ponds are an excellent source of irrigation, if you happen to have them close by. The water is free, there is no well to drill, and the amount of water is usually unlimited. Unfortunately, not many people have private ponds or streams within reach.

Cisterns

Cisterns have been in use for many years and can be found in the cellars of old houses. Space requirements might pose a problem, although there is no need for a lot of room. Depending on the intended use, the size of a storage tank might range from 100 to 1,000 gallons. Of course, the size of your irrigation project will determine the size of your cistern, but even if it won't handle all of your needs, it will help.

Water Tanks

Elevated water tanks are used to catch and hold rainwater. There aren't many people who live without electricity anymore, but there are more than you might imagine. In Maine, for instance, there are many people without power or running water. If you are in a situation where a pump is not practical, elevated holding tanks could be your answer. We will go into extensive detail on these various methods of irrigating your garden and lawn in the following chapters.

Code Requirements

There are government code requirements governing the installation of irrigation systems in most locations. The extent of these codes vary, but, in most cases, a permit is needed.

One of the most important code requirements is backflow protection, which was designed to prevent potable water systems from becoming contaminated. There are numerous situations where, without backflow protection, the water pipes for a building, including a municipal water system, could be rendered dangerous or deadly, not to mention useless. The exact mechanics of this are discussed in Chapter 9.

In addition to backflow protection, local code requirements probably will dictate the type of material to be used in your irrigation system. If the water source for your irrigation system is independent from the source for your drinking water, the requirements may not be as stringent. Law and regulation interpretations of the plumbing code and zoning ordinances vary from location to location. In any event, check with your local code-enforcement office prior to installing your irrigation system. This can save you a lot of grief down the road.

Covenants and Restrictions

Covenants and restrictions are often placed on properties in a subdivision in order for developers to maintain the integrity of their development. While it is highly unlikely that there will be any deed restrictions on installing an underground irrigation system, there could be prohibitions against aboveground systems. This is a point well worth looking into if you live in a structured development.

Zoning

Zoning requirements should not affect your decision to install an irrigation system, but they could. Ask officials in your town or city whether there are any zoning regulations that may restrict your irrigation plans.

Underground Utilities

If you plan to dig trenches for your new irrigation system, you must investigate the location of any underground utility lines. Digging up your telephone line will be frustrat-ing, not to mention costly, and digging up a high-voltage electric line or gas line could be deadly. A few phone calls to your local utility companies will determine whether there are any underground obstacles. If there are, most utility companies will send a representative out to mark those locations.

Property Boundaries

Property boundaries also could become an issue while installing an irrigation system. If you dig trenches or drill a well on someone else's property, you're going to have a problem, which probably will be costly. If there is any question about the location of your property lines, have them spotted by a surveyor before you begin any actual work.

Environmental Regulations

Environmental regulations most likely will not apply to your irrigation system, but then again, this could be another stumbling block to your plans. If you plan to irrigate near a pond, lake, river, or stream, check with your local agencies first to make sure you won't violate any environmental rule. The penalties for these violations can be steep.

Is Irrigation Practical?

I S IRRIGATION PRACTICAL FOR your lawn or garden? There are a number of factors to consider before this question can be answered. The idea of irrigation brings to mind many different methods. While one person may think of a simple lawn sprinkler and garden hose, someone else may envision pop-up lawn sprinklers, while yet another person might conjure an image of big hoses and pulsating nozzles spraying water for 100 feet. Irrigation methods and sources vary vastly, so deciding if a particular system is practical for your purpose requires a personal look at individual circumstances.

Unrolling a garden hose and connecting a sprinkler to it is something almost anyone can do. However, installing an underground sprinkler system with automatic controls and pop-up heads is quite a bit more expensive and definitely more complicated. Money is a key element in deciding on an irrigation system. After evaluating your needs, you may decide that investing a lot of cash in such equipment is a waste of your time and money. This chapter is going to help you sort out the mysteries surrounding irrigation decisions.

Financial Considerations

To get the best system you can afford, you have to do some advance planning, which is the key to a successful irrigation system that won't soak up all of your cash flow. One question to consider is whether or not you will need to borrow money.

Can You Justify the Cost?

One step is to design your dream system and then see if you can afford it. You may find that you've researched and planned a system that you can't afford, which is why it is wise to review your finances first and determine how much you can spend.

There are other factors to consider besides the cost of equipment, labor, and operating expenses. Can you justify spending a thousand dollars on an irrigation system that will be used only a couple of weeks a year? Can you justify to a lender that the improvement is worth its price? If gardening is your hobby, can you justify the cost as a hobby expense?

I'm not saying that you shouldn't or can't install an irrigation system if the numbers don't work, but it's necessary to have the needed information to make a sound decision. In view of this, let's run through some sample situations so that you can see how to evaluate the cost of your new system.

Assessing the Options: Example #1

Assume that you own a suburban home with a one-quarter acre of lawn. Your home is supplied with city water. In past years, you've watered your lawn with a standard lawn sprinkler and garden hose, but now you find that taking time out of your busy schedule to monitor the watering is bothersome. You want an irrigation system that will not consume so much time and attention.

In reflecting on past summers, you remember that your lawn needs watering about eight weeks out of the year to keep it lush. There have been times when your municipality has invoked watering bans, but these times are few and far between. Certainly not often enough

to justify the construction of a cistern or the drilling of an irrigation well. All you want is a simple way to water your lawn in a uniform fashion that will not eat away at your time. What are your options?

Option 1. You could opt for additional water hoses and sprinklers so that the entire lawn could be watered at one time. This, of course, is the least expensive option, but there are drawbacks. Having several hoses and sprinklers spread about your lawn will create an eyesore and require a lot of time setting them up and putting them away each day during the watering season. Since time is what you are trying to save, this approach is not very appealing.

Option 2. You could invest in a walking sprinkler, one that moves as it waters your lawn. The cost is modest, and you would need only one hose and one sprinkler. But, you'd still have to haul it in and out of the yard, and you'd have to be around to control the water flow to your lawn.

Option 3. You could install an underground sprinkler system. You've checked out these dream systems carefully and have fallen in love with the pop-up sprinkler heads, the automatic timer, and all the other goodies that go with the system. This is what you want, but you're not sure if you should spring for the major expense.

Decision time. If money were the only factor in these examples, multiple hoses and sprinklers would be the best option. However, money isn't the prime consideration; time is. The walking sprinkler is a fair compromise between the ultimate watering system and the simplest. Your heart is leading you to the underground system, but your bank account is forcing you to give serious consideration to the walking sprinkler.

During your evaluation, you look at the fact that your lawn is not very large. At first glance, the size of the area to be watered points to a walking sprinkler. On the other hand, since the yard isn't very big, the cost of installing an underground system wouldn't be staggering. Decisions, decisions, decisions.

Upon further research, you take into consideration that many of the homes in your area are equipped with pop-up sprinkler heads. Ah, there's some justification. Installing an underground system would enhance the value of your home and keep the exterior appearance on par with the other homes along

Attaching multiple hoses and sprinklers to outdoor faucets is the most inexpensive way to water an entire lawn, but it also creates an eyesore. Setting up the individual sprinklers and adjusting them every day is time-consuming as well. If you want to save time and improve the look of your lawn, you may want to consider installing an underground sprinkler system.

IS IRRIGATION PRACTICAL?

your street. Before making a commitment, you talk with neighbors who have underground systems. They all love their sprinklers. You're almost sold.

In the final phase of the decision-making process, you weigh other considerations. You don't plan to sell your home in the foreseeable future. If you were going to sell, it might make more sense to stick with a mobile system you could take with you, such as the walking sprinkler. Since time and appearance are of great concern to you, the nod goes to the underground sprinklers. You also rationalize that a sprinkler system will be more efficient than a hose sprinkler because you can carefully control the time and amount of watering, which will save you money each time the lawn is watered. You're getting very close to a commitment.

Justifying the cost. After pricing a complete underground system the cost is a little shocking. However, you decide that by installing the system yourself, the cost is bearable.

The determining factor in coming to a conclusion is how often the system will be used. If you average eight weeks a year, as you have in the past, the convenience of the underground system seems worth the cost. So, you buy the materials and install them.

This example is a fairly accurate account of how a decision might be reached about the type of irrigation system to install. Once you know what type of system you want, it is just a matter of finding enough good reasons to take the plunge. In this case, all of the supporting excuses for buying the most expensive system were good enough. But, suppose the system was to be used only two weeks each year. Could the decision still be made to install an underground system? It could be, but the justification would be lacking to some extent.

Assessing the Options: Example #2

Now let's look at a second example. In this situation, you love growing a vegetable garden each summer. You live in the country and the water to your house is supplied by a shallow well. During extremely dry periods, you must be careful not to run your well dry. Every year you water your garden with a garden hose when possible. It is your desire to create a better irrigation system for watering the vegetables. There is one problem: You only have $500 for a system.

In the last example, we focused on a desirable system first and then considered the cost. For this scenario, we are going to start with the available budget and work from that figure. What type of irrigation system can you create for $500 or less?

Cost considerations. Considering the amount of money available, several irrigation options are out. You can't afford to dig or drill a well. You could, however, have a driven well. Assuming you can hit water and obtain a satisfactory quantity, a driven point is inexpensive to install.

What are your other options? Running water from your home has been a problem: the well cannot always meet the demands of irrigation on top of your home water supply needs. One cost-effective idea is a cistern. A cistern, installed close to the garden plot, would do a bang-up job of watering all of your plants.

With a cistern, you can be assured of having water when you want it. The expense of building a cistern depends largely on whether you build it yourself — and the materials you choose to use — or whether you buy it. You could spend a lot of money on a custom-made masonry cistern, or you could take a cheaper route and purchase a used, aboveground swimming pool. Even some new pools will fit your budget. It is also possible that you could excavate an in-ground cistern for less than what your budget allows.

An inexpensive cistern. In this example, let's assume that you have ruled out the well point. You are considering a cistern; more specifically, a used swimming pool. I've seen aboveground pools advertised by owners who were willing to give them away to anyone who would disassemble the pool and haul it away. You can't beat a free cistern. New swimming pools to fit your needs are available for less than $200, which still leaves you with $300.

In addition to the pool, you will need a pump, a source of electricity, some pipe, and a distribution system. Having the cistern close to the garden allows you to use an inexpensive effluent (sump) pump, which costs less than $50. The pipe, even for a fairly long run, can be purchased for less than $25. So far you have spent $275 on your system.

Running electricity to the pump can be as simple as connecting a heavy-duty contractor-type extension cord between your house and the pump. Expect to spend about $30 for this. If the garden is more than 100 feet from your house, a good outdoor-grade sheathed wire, like you would use for a well pump, should be used. Even so, the cost will be under $50. You now have spent a total of $325. The only other thing you need is a distribution system.

Polybutylene (PB) piping is very inexpensive and extremely effective in irrigation uses. I use it almost exclusively in all of my plumbing jobs. A ½-inch PB pipe costs 22¢ per foot.

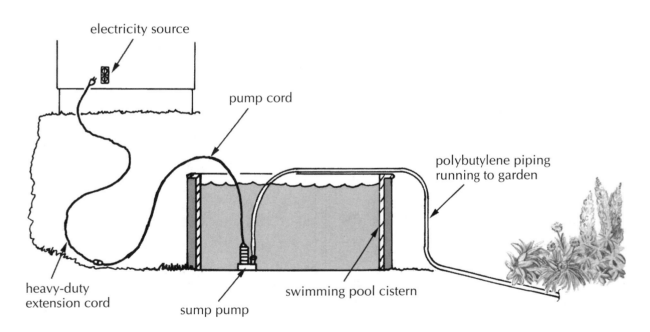

electricity source

pump cord

polybutylene piping
running to garden

heavy-duty
extension cord

sump pump

swimming pool cistern

An inexpensive cistern watering system can be made from a used swimming pool with an effluent (sump) pump. Set the pool up close to the garden so that the pump's power is adequate for meeting the garden's water needs.

IS IRRIGATION PRACTICAL?

Even with a large garden, it is unlikely that you would use more than 300 feet of piping to distribute your water. If you round the numbers up to $25 per 100-foot roll, the cost of 300 feet is only $75. Now you are at a total of $400 for your irrigation system. After throwing in a few miscellaneous fittings, you may hit a grand total of $425, which still is well within your $500 budget. See how easy this is?

You now have seen two different approaches to planning a budget for your irrigation system. I'm sure you can come up with some variations, but the examples should give you some insight into how you can have an adequate irrigation system.

As you probably know, money is not the only factor to be considered when thinking of an irrigation system. Physical limitations play a large role in what is and is not feasible.

Topography Limitations

Topography limitations can be an obstacle when planning an irrigation system. For instance, at the site of the new home I'm building, my irrigation need is to water our horses. The barn is about 250 feet away from the house. Carrying water to the barn from the house is not a fun prospect, especially in sub-zero temperatures and three feet of snow. I want to install a bury-hydrant at the barn in order to have running water all through the year, but I have a problem.

The topography of my land is not conducive to a uniform trench. Dips in the land mean that in order to lay pipe below the frost line, which is four feet deep in this part of the state, I will have to lay it nearly seven feet deep in some places. In addition to this, the land is

laden with rocks and bedrock. As much as I want a buried, year-round water line to the barn, I may not be able to have it. This same type of problem can crop up when you are planning your irrigation system.

In an earlier example, I mentioned a farmer who was considering an in-ground cistern. If the land around the garden plot was like my land, solid rock, an in-ground cistern would not be feasible, unless blasting were to take place. Blasting is an expensive proposition, and usually is not a justifiable expense for small-scale irrigation systems.

Deed Restrictions

Covenants and restrictions in the deed to your property may stipulate what can and cannot be constructed on the property. For instance, my parents are limited in the colors they can use to paint the exterior of their home and restricted by the types of vehicles they can park in their driveway, among other things. These types of recorded restrictions can limit your options greatly, and, as mentioned earlier, need to be researched before choosing any irrigation system.

When investigating your irrigation options, try to consider as many elements as possible. Will the system freeze, creating a need for a system that can be removed before winter? Are there any underground utilities in the path of your irrigation system that might cause a problem? Is an overhead irrigation system for your garden a good idea? Would a cistern make an ideal water source for your needs? How much is it going to cost to use metered city water for your irrigation purposes? As you can see, there are countless questions to ask, and ask you should. It is your job to plan, design, develop, and install the most effective system within your budget.

Frequency Of Use

As mentioned earlier, the frequency of use should be a factor in considering how much money to invest in an irrigation system. Obviously, where you live will play a big part in how often you rely on irrigation equipment to keep your grass green and your corn tall. Some places are hotter and drier than others. In Maine, irrigation is negligible: Hot weather usually invades the state only for a few weeks each year, and the rainfall rate in Maine is high. Virginia, on the other hand, where I grew up, is much hotter and drier. I can remember it being so hot during summer months that the tar on the roads would melt and stick to the bottoms of my shoes. The garden soil would turn to dust. Grass would burn and turn brown from the heat. There was a definite need for irrigation.

The Personal Factor: So What if the Watermelon is Puny?

What's a puny watermelon to anyone? So what if it's been hot and dry and the melon patch shrivels and dies? Who cares? Well, to a lot of people, gardening is very important. Professional farmers must make the most of their crops, but why are homeowners so concerned about their gardens? Really, if you look at a small vegetable garden with a feasibility study, it's hard to justify. When you factor in all the money spent on tilling the soil, buying seeds, and adding growing agents, how much money is saved when compared to buying vegetables from the local grocer? Continue the study by putting a value on the time you work in the garden, and the justification dwindles. Since a small garden is probably not a profitable venture to begin with, why would anyone spend additional money on an irrigation system? There can only be one reason: personal satisfaction.

Lawns and gardens are therapeutic for many people. If you come home from a stressful day at the office, an hour in your garden can relax and refresh you. It restores your perspective on life and takes you back in time, to a simpler life. You can achieve a similar feeling as you sit in the shade and admire the lush lawn that rivals the best putting greens around. Your green thumb has created something of which you are proud, something that you enjoy, and something that only you understand best. If you share these types of feelings, an irrigation system should be in your future.

Freshwater Sources

THERE ARE SEVERAL WAYS TO obtain a freshwater source for your irrigation needs. The simplest source is a municipal water supply, if it is available. Additional sources of freshwater include drilled wells, dug wells, and driven wells. If you have modern plumbing, you have a source of freshwater right under your roof.

Chapter 2 gave you a brief introduction to various water sources and irrigation methods. This chapter provides technical information needed to make a wise irrigation decision. Since irrigation requires a water source, there is no better place to start than with the options for water.

Potable Water

Water used for drinking, cooking, and bathing is potable water. Water used for irrigation purposes isn't necessarily potable, but it can be, especially if you have an abundant supply of potable water. In Chapter 4, we'll look at nonpotable sources suitable for irrigation.

Normally potable water is derived from municipal or private well systems. Sometimes it is taken from springs in the ground.

Municipal Water Systems

Municipal water systems offer advantages for watering. The two most obvious are the ready access to an abundant water supply and the fact that tapping into the water source from within your home doesn't incur much additional cost. I can think of only two disadvantages associated with using city water for irrigation. One is that you may be limited in regards to when and how often you can use a public water source for irrigation. The other is the cost you may be charged for metered water.

Assuming that your home is connected to a public water service and that you are willing to pay so much per gallon for its use in irrigation, you are pretty well set. All you have to do is cut a tee fitting into the main water supply within your home, and you're in business. (See Chapter 9 for instructions.)

Driven Wells

Plumbers often refer to driven wells as *points*. They talk about *driving a point*, which means creating a well. We know that point wells are inexpensive, but there is more to consider before running out and buying equipment to sink your own well.

Finding Water

Finding water to drive your point can be the most difficult challenge in creating a driven well. If the water table in your area is low, a driven well may not be practical. Call your local county Cooperative Extension Service office, or some similar agency, to request information on water levels in your area.

There is no rule of thumb for determining when a water table is too deep for a driven point since other factors affect its feasibility. For example, if your soil is loose and sandy, you can drive a point to great depths. A rocky ledge, however, will prevent any reasonable possibility for using a driven point.

You can get some idea of soil conditions by digging a hole with a shovel or by driving a steel rod into the ground. Before doing either, make sure there are no underground utilities. Surface water running near the top of the earth is one indicator of a good drive point. Once you've determined that your soil allows the use of a driven point, you can begin to install the well, for which you will need some specific equipment and materials.

Acquiring Supplies and Equipment

The well point and accessories are available at some, but not all, plumbing suppliers, so call to make sure the items you need are in stock before going to pick them up.

The tools needed for this job include: a sledgehammer, a stepladder, and a pipe wrench or large pliers. You will also need a drive tip to attach to the first section of the point shaft that will be driven into the ground. Depending on the expected depth of your well, you also will need several sections of point shafts — tubes with fine slits cut into them. Once the point shaft is below the water table, water runs into the slits and fills the shaft. The shaft retains water for pumping as long as the slits remain below the water table.

Shaft sections for well points are normally sold in 5- and 10-foot sections. The shorter sections are easier to manipulate. It is also possible to buy the shafts made from either steel or Schedule-40 plastic. Both will work in soft ground, but metal shafts tend to do better in rocky spots.

To join the shaft sections together, you will need drive couplings, which provide a surface to hammer the point as it is driven so as not to damage the threaded ends of the shaft. As each section is driven into the ground, a new section can be added by threading it into a coupling.

Driving the Point

Once you have all your gear, you're ready to drive your point. Attach the drive cap to the drive point. Some sections of drive points come with the first shaft section. Pick your place on the ground and place the drive point on it. If you're tall and your ground is soft, you may not need a ladder when working with 5-foot drive sections, but it may be easier to work from a stepladder.

With the drive point in place, use a heavy hammer (at least six pounds) to drive the point into the earth. When the drive cap gets close to the ground, install a second section of drive shaft. Also install a drive cap on the remaining threads of the new shaft. Continue this process until the shaft cannot be driven any further. The deeper the shaft is driven, the more likely you are to hit a vein of water that will produce during dry spells.

When you have driven your last section of point, you are ready to install the piping for your pump. You will want to check to make sure you have hit water before hooking up a pump. To do this, drop a line with something

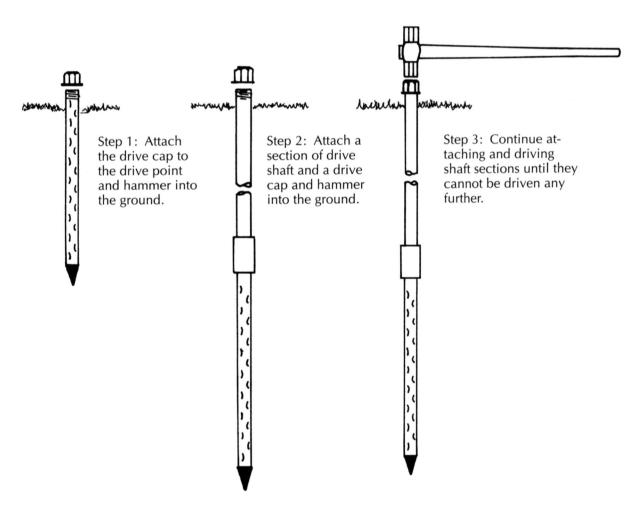

Step 1: Attach the drive cap to the drive point and hammer into the ground.

Step 2: Attach a section of drive shaft and a drive cap and hammer into the ground.

Step 3: Continue attaching and driving shaft sections until they cannot be driven any further.

A driven well is created by driving a point into soil where you've determined water is likely to be found. You can drive it yourself with a sledgehammer and some muscle strength.

on the end of it (like a weighted cotton ball or the nut from a bolt) down the point to test for water in the shaft. After it hits bottom, pull the string up and see if it is wet. You can also determine how high your water column is from the length of wetness on the string.

Pros and Cons of Driven Wells

The drawbacks of driven wells may be great enough to make you turn your attention to some other type of well or water source. First of all, you may drive several points without finding water, and if you do locate water, there is no guarantee how much volume you will be able to pump without depleting the supply. When your irrigation plans call for a substantial amount of water, this can be a very real problem.

Limited Water Production

Due to the nature of a driven well, you cannot expect too much water production. The well shaft is very small, and the point is not likely to hit a major vein of water with a high gpm rating. Also, there is not enough volume of water maintained in the point shaft to keep up with heavy usage from irrigation equipment. If you want to water a small garden once a day, a driven well will probably work fine, but don't expect to water a large lawn repetitively without problems.

On the other hand, I know of several homes in Maine where a driven point is the only source of water. Most of the locations have sandy soil, so the points were easy to drive into decent water levels. The owners of these homes use water from their points all

year and don't experience problems with water quantity. While driven points cannot be relied on to provide adequate water for large residential irrigation projects, there are many times when a point can serve your needs.

Another common problem with a driven well is the slits in the point shafts becoming blocked with debris and sediment, preventing water from entering the shaft. Ultimately, this results in a lack of water and a need to drive a new point. Aside from these potential drawbacks, driven wells can give good service.

Advantages Over Dug and Drilled Wells

There is no comparison between a driven well and a dug or drilled well. The advantages of the first far exceed those of the others: Driven points are small, easy to install, and inexpensive. These facts make a driven well worth considering.

Given the low cost of installing a driven well, it is easy to justify the cost of several driven wells in different locations. You might have one for your garden and another for watering your lawn. It is also possible to drive multiple points in various locations to hedge against running out of water. If you have a driven well that doesn't produce a heavy volume of water at one time, but replenishes itself well, you can pump into a storage tank, which will give you plenty of volume when you need it, without putting a strain on your well.

Dug Wells

Dug wells are very common in southern states, but not in the Northeast. I've owned three homes served by dug wells. Only one of the wells didn't keep up with my needs for water, due, in part, to a large, whirlpool tub that consumed hundreds of gallons of water each week. The well did fine most of the time, but there were occasions when it ran empty. The bad times were always in the heat of a Virginia summer, obviously, and this is when irrigation water is needed most.

If your home is served by a dug well, you can use the water for your house *and* your irrigation needs, although you may find that it cannot handle the demands you are putting on it. On the other hand, I have seen shallow (dug) wells that were impossible to run dry.

As a home builder and plumber, I have had a wealth of experience with wells. In the early days, I climbed inside old, hand-dug wells lined with rock, which was not one of the more glamorous sides of plumbing. I never knew what kind of creepy crawlers might be laying on the next rock as I descended into the dark depths. Modern dug wells are lined with round concrete sleeves instead of rocks. Also, it is no longer necessary to climb into wells to work on pumps and related equipment, fortunately.

When a house is built and a well is used for water, the well must be disinfected and tested for bacteria. This is usually done by pouring chlorine bleach into the drinking water and letting it set for a while. Next, the water is drained out of the well, and the reserve chamber is allowed to refill with fresh water. I've built houses where we could never get the shallow wells to run dry. In some cases, we ran as many faucets as we could for over 12 hours without eliminating the supply of water in the well. So, there is really no way to know if a dug well will have trouble producing a high volume of water or not. You have to base your

decision on averages, and, on average, a shallow well is likely to have problems maintaining a large demand for water during hot, dry summer months.

I won't advise you not to install your own dug well, but I won't recommend it. In my opinion, all well drilling and digging operations should be left to professionals, with the exception of driven wells. You can install your own pump and piping, but leave the earth work to the pros.

Pros And Cons of Dug Wells

Dug wells offer several advantages over drilled wells. First, they are considerably less expensive to create. If you hit a good vein of water, a dug well can produce a high quantity of water on demand. The cost of installing a pump and piping is less for a dug well than for a drilled well. Installing a pump in a dug well also is easier than installing a submersible pump in a drilled well.

Now for the disadvantages. Dug wells sometimes run out of water. You can never be guaranteed of hitting water when creating a well, but the odds of striking a usable quantity of water are better when the well is drilled, rather than dug. Dug wells have much larger diameters than drilled wells, which means they take up more space. An average dug well will have a diameter of about 3 feet; a drilled well will not be more than 6 inches in diameter. If, for any reason, the top is left off a dug well, you have created an instant death trap. Dug wells are large enough to swallow an adult, child, or pet. Sediment also can be cause for concern in a dug well. As time passes, sediment can invade the well and make it shallower. In extreme cases, this can render the well useless.

All in all, dug wells are a pretty good source of irrigation water, the caveat being water quantity. If you will need extensive amounts of water for prolonged periods of time, however, a dug well is not a wise idea. Under such conditions, a drilled well is the way to go.

Drilled Wells

Installing a drilled well is definitely beyond the capability of most homeowners. These wells usually are drilled with rigs costing hundreds of thousands of dollars, and you can't just run down to the rental store and get one for the weekend.

Pros and Cons of Drilled Wells

Drilled wells require very little space on the surface of the earth. Their small-diameter pipe is unobtrusive and generally presents little risk to people. The depth of a drilled well can vary a great deal. A well drilled on one side of your property may go down 150 feet to hit an aquifer capable of yielding a flow rate of 5 gpm, while a second well at another location on the same property may result in a depth of 300 feet or more.

Drilled wells are expensive but almost never run dry, and the chances of hitting a satisfactory water vein are extremely good, due to the depth possibility of the well. While the cost of a drilled well is probably twice that of a dug well, there are some assurances when drilling.

There are two approaches to hiring a well driller. You can pay the driller on a per-foot basis or on a flat-rate basis. The per-foot basis is more risky, because you have no way of knowing the depth of the well. However, I've taken this gamble on many occasions and always won, so far. That's not to say, though, that agreeing to a per-foot deal is the best method.

When you contract a well driller on a flat-rate basis, you are guaranteed water at a minimum flow rate, usually 3 gpm. Even if the driller hits a dry hole and has to start over, you're only paying the contracted amount. By hiring the work in this manner, you can budget and control the cost of your well. Taking the gamble on a per-foot basis could result in a well that costs much more than you or the driller anticipated. Even though I have gambled, I would recommend that you settle on a firm contract price and reduce your risk.

Apart from the costs of a drilled well and a submersible pump system, it is hard to find any disadvantages to this method.

~ 4 ~

Recycling Water for Irrigation

FRESHWATER IS NOT A NECESSITY for irrigation. You might consider recycling water for irrigation purposes. Depending upon where you live, there may be many ways to obtain water for irrigating your lawn and garden without drilling a well or paying exorbitant water bills.

People in past centuries often settled near a natural water source, such as a lake or stream. This was fine when there was ample unsettled land with water and fewer people looking for a place to live. Today, however, while there are still private homes situated near natural water sources, most people don't have a waterfront view.

Obviously, having a pond, lake, or stream in your backyard is an easy way to get irrigation water. You run a pipe into the water source, connect it to a pump, and you're in

business. Even if you don't have this option, there are a number of creative ways to collect water for irrigation purposes.

My sixty-four-acre farm has a good pond, a dug well for livestock, and a drilled well for the house. Water is not much of a problem. I'm also in the process of building a new house on much less acreage, but the land has 800 feet of river frontage, a good pond, and some springs and streams. Again, water shouldn't be a problem. I am lucky to have such abundant, free, water sources. However, I realize not all people are so fortunate.

Some methods explored in this chapter won't be practical for people living in the city. Other methods will cater to the needs of people with limited space. Even if your garden is in a window box, you'll find some nuggets of information worth remembering.

Ponds and Lakes

Ponds and lakes are ideal sources of irrigation water. Whether created by nature or by humans, ponds and lakes can provide more than enough water for even large-scale irrigation. If one of these water sources is in the vicinity of your lawn or garden, you've got it made.

Getting water from the pond or lake to the irrigation area is usually pretty simple. Since you won't be irrigating during freezing weather, the piping can be above the frost line and installed temporarily. Very little is required in the way of materials.

~ ~ ~ ~ ~

Pump Installation in a Pond or Lake

1. The pump and pressure tank must be located near the irrigation site.

2. You will need only 110 volts of electricity.

3. To begin, attach the well pipe to the pump and run the pipe to the water source — it is okay for the pipe to lay on top of the ground.

4. Install a foot valve on the pipe end to be submerged in the water. This valve acts as a strainer and a check valve, to keep your pump from losing its prime. Allow enough length on the pipe so that it will remain submerged under the water. Do not let the end of the pipe and the foot valve rest on a sandy or muddy bottom. You will need to install gauges, relief valves, cut-off valves, and various fittings as described in Chapter 5.

5. Once the pipe is under the water, you are ready to prime the pump.

To do this, remove the priming plug and pour water into the priming hole until the well pipe and pump body are full.

6. Replace the priming plug and you are ready to turn on the pump and energize your pressure tank. A pipe connects your irrigation system to the pressure tank and provides a constant flow of water on demand.

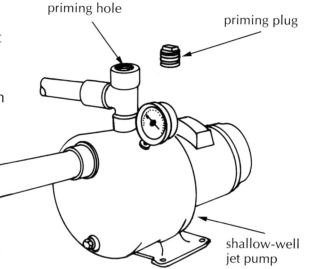

priming hole

priming plug

shallow-well jet pump

Pumping water is discussed extensively in Chapter 5, but in this chapter I cover the basic requirements of getting water from various sources to the irrigation site.

Pump System

Setting up a pump system for a pond or lake requires a shallow-well pump, also called a jet pump. If you want to increase water pressure and reduce wear and tear on the pump, you will need a pressure tank and the necessary fittings. You will also need a coil of plastic well pipe. The last major component is a foot valve.

Installing this type of system is quite simple and relatively inexpensive; one person can accomplish it in only a few hours. No exotic tools or equipment is needed. There are, however, a few pointers I'd like to pass on to you. While the next chapter will educate you about pumps, it will not warn you of the difficulties you may encounter when pumping water from a pond or lake, so I'd like to do that now.

Protecting the Foot Valve

The bottoms of many ponds and lakes consist of mud, silt, sand, or a combination of the three. These elements can plug up a foot valve very quickly. If this happens, the pump will run, but no water (or very little water) will be supplied to the pressure tank. This

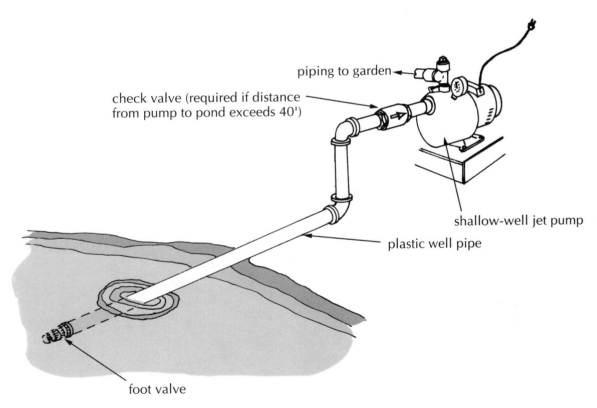

piping to garden

check valve (required if distance from pump to pond exceeds 40')

shallow-well jet pump

plastic well pipe

foot valve

A simple seasonal pumping system can be set up from a pond or lake near your garden with a shallow-well jet pump and some plastic well pipe. Once the season's over, the system can be easily disassembled, so you don't need to worry about frozen pipes.

RECYCLING WATER FOR IRRIGATION

situation normally doesn't occur when the foot valve is suspended in the water and not near contaminants. In a lake or pond, however, the foot valve often sinks to the bottom. Unless the body of water has a steep bank that drops off suddenly, there is no way to avoid this.

One simple, inexpensive method to keep a foot valve from coming into contact with the bottom of a pond or lake, however, is to build a box frame covered with screen wire to enclose the foot valve. The frame of the box can be made with scrap lumber and covered with any type of fine-mesh screen. With the foot valve protected by the screen box, you won't have to worry about it plugging up. There may be occasions when you will need to pull the pipe out of the water and clean debris, such as leaves and weeds, from the sides of the box, but you will avoid the aggravation and expense of having your foot valve plugged up every time you put it in the water.

If your lake or pond has a dock extending out into it, you can suspend the well pipe and foot valve from the side of the dock. This will position the foot valve vertically in the water so that it functions just as it would in a well. Keep the foot valve several feet off of the bottom of the lake or pond to prevent it from sucking in particles that could restrict its function. Either method will make your system work better, and neither will add much cost to your job.

Moving Water

Moving water, such as streams and rivers, is a good source of irrigation, but requires a few compensating techniques to overcome the water's movement. If you've ever gone fishing in moving water while using a fishing float, you know how the current often carries it downstream — frequently right into one of

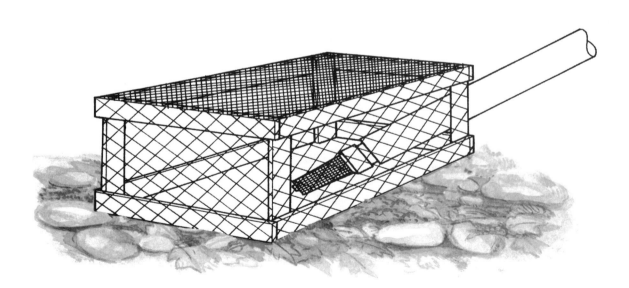

You can build a simple, inexpensive screened box from scrap lumber and wire mesh to protect the foot valve from becoming clogged with debris from the lake or pond bottom. The box also serves as an anchor.

WATERING SYSTEMS FOR LAWN AND GARDEN

the tributary's banks if you let it go long enough. This same thing can happen to your well pipe and foot valve. Depending on the strength of the river current, you will need to anchor your foot valve in place.

Protecting the Foot Valve

River and stream water is a conduit for floating debris. Just as I advised you to protect your foot valve from the bottoms of ponds and lakes, you should also protect it in moving water. The screened box described on the previous page can serve two purposes in moving water: preventing the foot valve from picking up foreign particles; and, with added weight, acting as an anchor. The added weight can be a brick, a cinderblock, or even an old piece of chain wrapped around the frame. Of course, you could invest in a small mushroom anchor (like the ones used for canoes and small boats) if you want a first-class job. If your source of moving water is clogged with tree branches, roots, and other tangles, a mushroom anchor is a good investment. Chains, cinderblocks, and similar homemade weights may get tangled in underwater obstacles and prevent you from being able to retrieve your foot valve.

Springs

Springs are another natural source of irrigation water. Not all springs produce large quantities of water, but some do. My pond is spring fed, and its water level rarely drops, even in extremely dry periods. I know of a spring where people drive from miles around to fill their plastic jugs. This spring runs all the time, and it is not unusual to see a line of people waiting to fill dozens of milk jugs. The flow from this particular spring is similar to the flow from a ½-inch pipe with its faucet turned about halfway on. The flow certainly wouldn't fill out a fire hose, but with a pressure tank and pump, it would do a dandy job of watering a garden.

Many springs dry up during the hot summer months, which is a problem if you rely on the spring for your irrigation needs. However, most any spring will produce water in the early part of the summer and in the fall. Any water you can get from a spring is free water, not to mention that you could build a water storage system and take full benefit of the spring's output before it dries up in the late summer.

Digging Out a Spring

One way to increase the reserve capability of a spring is to dig it out. Your excavation can be as much or as little as you like. If you're so inclined and have the space and the money, you can build a spring-fed pond. This is probably overkill for most folks, but it's worth mentioning.

If you dig a spring hole, line the sides of the hole to prevent erosion and settling that will fill the spring with dirt and debris. How you line the hole depends on how big it is. Well casing, like that used with dug wells, makes a great (but heavy) lining for your spring hole. A 55-gallon drum can be used if you cut out the ends. The metal drum will have to be replaced periodically, but it doesn't weigh much, and one person can install it easily. Plywood also can be used and it, too, will have to be replaced from time to time. As long as the liner protects the hole from cave-ins, it's doing its job.

Selecting a Pond Site and Estimating Its Potential

When you think about it, it's not surprising that natural ponds almost never form in coarse soils that drain well. Yet thousands of attempts at man-made ponds in just such places have proven to be dismal failures. A good pond takes careful research.

Clay is thought to be ideal for a pond bottom. But it's not without its disadvantages. Very waterproof and stable when dry, overly steep clay banks can slide toward flatness when wet. A clay bottom is slippery and soggy, not particularly fun to walk in. When disturbed, it turns water murky.

At the opposite extreme, bedrock — or ledge — is next to impossible to excavate without blasting. Besides, it's pierced with cracks and fissures that can leak forever. Ponds can be expensively lined with plastic membranes, high-density concrete, or clay. But the ideal soil condition is somewhere between clay and rock: good digging in predictable earth that may leak a trifle at first, but will eventually seal itself with silt and sediment.

Topographical depressions, swampy valleys, and wet spots are often good pond sites, just as long as the soil base will hold water. In many parts of the country, the U.S. Soil Conservation Service will help you design and lay out a pond at little or no cost, and be able to tell you if you have enough water and enough of the right kind of soil for a particular type of pond construction.

Estimating pond capacity. If a pond holds enough to supply a farm or homestead with a year's worth of water — beyond what evaporates and leaks out — a pond is thought to be big enough. Its potential is best figured during the driest part of the year — in August or early September in most places. Calculating the pond's acre footage, with the help of rectangular measurements at the pond site and sketches on graph paper, is a help in estimating the pond's storage capacity. An acre foot is the water needed to cover one acre (43,560 square feet), one foot deep. There are about 325,851 gallons per acre foot. Unless the water table nearby is exceptionally high, each acre foot of pond may receive water from 1½ to 2 acres of watershed. Obviously if the watershed falls short of the pond's needs, the pond never fills.

Excerpted from *The Home Water Supply* by Stu Campbell (Garden Way Publishing, 1983).

A natural spring is a good source of water for a small lawn or garden, but don't expect an average spring to meet the demands of heavy irrigation, which only can be done when the spring has been enlarged to create a sizable reservoir, or when the water is stored in some other location.

Cisterns

People used to divert rainwater from their roofs into a holding pool or cistern. There are still numerous homes in Maine with cisterns under them. While it is unlikely you will put a cistern in your basement or cellar, you might want to consider building one near your irrigation site.

The term *cistern* encompasses a broad range of possibilities. Depending on your interpretation, a cistern could be a 55-gallon drum, a water tank set up on legs, or the equivalent of a swimming pool. Technically, I suppose a coffee can set under the corner of your roof could pass for a cistern. Depending upon your age, you might well remember the rain barrels of old. It was not uncommon to see these barrels set in strategic locations to capture rainwater. These too could be considered a type of cistern.

Probably the best-known cistern is a container with a round shape, walls that rise a couple of feet above the bottom, and no top. It looks something like a wading pool for children. This type of cistern can hold a lot of water, and was often used in older homes for reserve water.

Building a cistern near your garden provides many benefits: You can catch and store free water; you will not have far to pump the water; and, depending upon how you build

the container, you can use it to cool off on hot days. The main advantage is having a ready source of water close to your point of need.

Building a Garden Pond Cistern

Building a cistern today is easier in some ways and more complicated in others than it was years ago. Most building codes today treat any holding vessel with a depth for water exceeding 18 inches as a swimming pool. This definition may open a number of regulatory issues involving special fencing and other local requirements. Before building a cistern, check with your local code enforcement office for area rules and regulations.

Old cisterns usually were made from rock or concrete. With today's new membrane linings and materials, it is possible to build one without all those heavy materials. In fact, you can build the cistern either above or below ground level. It can even double as a decorative fish pond or a place for the kids to splash around. If you want to keep your construction time to a minimum, you can purchase a used, aboveground swimming pool to use as your holding vessel.

When I built my last house in Virginia, I installed a cistern of sorts. It was a contemporary-style home on five acres, affording us a great deal of privacy and a lot of lawn. We also created a garden spot on part of the land. Virginia can have some really hot, humid, dry summers, and we were concerned about our watering needs. We had a shallow well, which was standard practice in our part of the state. Having just moved from a house with a shallow well, we knew about the limitations of irrigating.

Rather than spend a lot of money drilling a well or installing a separate shallow well, we decided to create a garden pond. This decorative pond made a beautiful addition to the grounds while serving as our source of irrigation.

As a building contractor, I was lucky to have friends with muscle willing to help us. I threw a little work party for our construction crew, and we had the pond dug in one day, by hand.

Most of the pond was no more than 2 feet deep. We dug the hole by hand and lined it with inexpensive tarp, the kind that costs about twenty dollars. After fitting the tarp into the hole and securing the top edge with tent stakes, we filled the pond with enough well water to hold the tarp in place.

We put fish in the water, and my wife created a water garden with various types of plants. The garden pond was only a few feet deep at its deepest end, but it gave the fish a place of retreat in freezing weather.

Basically the pond was a cistern, a holding vessel for stored water. As the rains came, the pond filled up. Then it was just a matter of occasional maintenance to keep it full.

Whenever the lawn or the garden needed watering, I put a submersible sump pump into the pond and pumped water through a garden hose. The pump plugged into an outside electrical outlet on the side of the house. By using a sump pump and garden hose, my irrigation costs were negligible. To demonstrate how little this type of irrigation system can cost, let me give you a basic rundown of the materials needed. The estimated costs of these supplies are detailed in the box.

You will need a tarp large enough to cover the bottom, sides, and ends of your pool. If

You can create a good water source by digging a 2-foot deep garden pond and lining it with an inexpensive tarp. Secure the tarp with stakes before filling the cistern with water. Once full, the pond can be landscaped with plantings and other decorative features.

WATERING SYSTEMS FOR LAWN AND GARDEN

the pool is 2 feet deep, a 20-foot by 30-foot tarp will accommodate a pool 26 feet by 16 feet, which is a pretty good-sized garden pool. You'll also need tent stakes to secure the top of the tarp.

The digging is done with a shovel, so there is no monetary outlay needed for this phase of the job. The next cost is for a sump pump. I recommend a submersible one that discharges through a garden hose and runs on 110-volt electricity. This little pump produces 1,200 gallons of water per hour when it is pumping a head of water 5 feet high. Since you will not be pumping more than 2 or 3 feet if your pool is only 2 feet deep, you will get a little more output. You'll also need a good quality 50-foot garden hose.

This type of cistern fits into most settings. Whether you have a home in the suburbs or

The Cost of Building a Garden Pond

Assuming the pond is dug by hand, the cost of supplies is very reasonable. Following are 1996 estimated costs:

Supply	Estimated Cost
20' x 30' tarp	$20
Tent stakes	$10
Submersible sump pump	$50
50-foot garden hose (good quality)	$20
Total Cost of Supplies	$100

When you're ready to water your lawn or garden from your garden pond, simply put a submersible sump pump into the pond and pump water through a garden hose. Once you're done, remove the pump and hose to restore the pristine look of your pond.

RECYCLING WATER FOR IRRIGATION

the country, a garden pond adds appeal to your grounds and provides a good source of irrigation water. You can make the watering hole as decorative as you like and still have an adequate irrigation system.

Other Options

Not all cisterns have to be a garden pond. If your garden is in a place where the appearance of your cistern is not important, you can build the holding tank in a number of ways. Following are some cost-effective ideas for constructing your water reserve.

Many cisterns sit above ground. If you don't mind the appearance, a used, above-ground swimming pool is an excellent idea.

Even if the filters and other pool accessories are in bad condition, you can have a fantastic cistern, and you should be able to drive a hard bargain on the price of the unit.

Recently I was looking for a wading pool for my daughter and came across an above-ground pool, 3-feet deep, with a large circumference, about 12 feet in diameter. This particular pool came complete with filtering equipment and was priced less than $200. When considering the volume of water that can be stored in such a pool, there is no question it would be quite effective.

Depending on how primitive you are willing to get, you could line up a bunch of 55-gallon drums to store water, which is not as convenient as having all the water in one container, but serves the purpose.

If cost is not a consideration, you could hire a concrete company to build a cistern. The concrete would have to be sealed to avoid leakage, and the job would be expensive, but there would be no limitations on size and shape.

This set-up is useful for filling a cistern that is a distance from your house. Rainwater from your house's downspouts can be collected in a barrel and pumped via a sump pump to your cistern.

In my opinion, the two best methods of building a cistern storage system are to use an aboveground swimming pool or to install an in-ground garden pond. If your home is in a subdivision with covenants and restrictions, the garden pond may be the only option.

Filling Your Cistern

Filling your cistern with water can be done in scores of ways. You could hire a company that trucks water for swimming pools. This, of course, is costly. The cistern can be filled with well water or city water. In the case of city water, you still are facing a water bill. With well water, your only cost is the electricity used to run the pump.

Provided that you build your cistern early in the growing season, nature will contribute greatly to filling the container, which you can help in a number of ways. If your house is equipped with gutters and downspouts, you have an excellent source of water if it is possible to make a direct connection between your downspouts and the holding tank.

If your downspout is not close to your cistern, you still can make adaptations. Assuming your house is equipped with gutters and downspouts, but your cistern is too far away and too high to allow rainwater to run directly into the holding tank, you could pipe your downspouts to a miniature cistern (a 5-gallon bucket or a 55-gallon drum, for instance). Then the collected water could be pumped to the cistern with an inexpensive effluent (sump) pump, as illustrated.

While catching rainwater from your roof may seem like a slow method to get irrigation water, you will be surprised how fast it accumulates. I left a large contractor's wheelbarrow under the corner of my roof one night, and a small thunderstorm filled it to overflowing — that's several gallons of water. If there were a rain barrel under each gutter outlet, it's hard to predict how much water would accumulate.

Rain plays a significant role in filling a cistern, but you cannot count solely on the rain to be sufficient for your watering purposes. Run-off water from the roof of your home is only one way of meeting this demand. Supplementing water in the cistern with well water or city water is another way to maintain your high-water mark. A driven well point can also produce enough water to keep your cistern at a high level.

However you keep the cistern full of water, you can enjoy the low cost of using an effluent pump with this type of system. The vertical rise of water being pumped is so low that a jet pump is not needed. This fact alone will save you hundreds of dollars in start-up costs.

RECYCLING WATER FOR IRRIGATION

Selecting and Installing a Pump

PUMPING WATER FOR AN IRRIGA-
tion system can be complex
and costly, but it doesn't have
to be. With the proper under-
standing of how pumps work and an efficient
design for your irrigation piping, the cost and
complexity of pumping water can be kept at
a minimum.

It's important to understand how the
various types of water pumps work, and
what the differences are between effluent
pumps, single-pipe jet pumps, dual-pipe jet
and submersible deep-well pumps. It is
even possible to use the pump that serves
the water distribution system of your home
as an irrigation pump.

Any one of the pumps mentioned above
might best suit your needs. If you had to
guess right now, what type of pump would
you think is best for irrigation purposes? In

general, a deep-well submersible pump is
the best, but there are circumstances when
it is not the best choice for lawn and garden
irrigation. This is good news, because deep-
well pumps and their installation requirements are expensive. It is very likely that
you can use your existing water pump or an
inexpensive effluent pump to water your
lawn and garden.

If you use a municipal water system, you
may decide that a pump is not needed for
your irrigation purposes. The water provided
by your community can be piped directly to
your irrigation points, but there is a catch:
You may find that the water bill from your
town or city is too high to justify watering
your lawn or garden as often as you would
like. If this is the case, you might want to consider using an alternative water source and
pump just for your irrigation needs; so even

if you get your water from a municipal source, read on.

Selecting a Pump

Being a master plumber in a rural location, I work with all types of water pumps on a regular basis. My many years of hands-on experience with pumps has proven very helpful for designing irrigation systems and putting them into operation. Reading this chapter will not make you a master plumber, but it will give you more knowledge about pumps than many plumbers possess. While I won't go into great detail on troubleshooting and repairing pumps, I will provide an in-depth look at the common types of pumps available and how you can make a wise choice in the type that will serve your needs best.

Picking the right pump for irrigation purposes takes some thought. There are several questions you must ask yourself before you run out and buy one. For instance, what type of water source will you be using? Chapter 3 discusses the options for freshwater sources, and Chapter 4 examines the possibilities for using recycled water. The source of your irrigation water will have much to do with the type of pump you buy.

If you're already using a pump for your home water supply, you may be able to tap into it for irrigation purposes. However, before trying to save a few dollars by using your household pump, there are other considerations involved. For example, straining your well and pump to irrigate your lawn or garden could result in a burned-out pump or a depleted water supply in your well. This is serious and costly business that should not be taken lightly. However, it does not require highly technical knowledge to make a good choice.

You can learn enough about pumps from this chapter to make a sound buying decision. It is not important to understand all the technical aspects of pumps, such as centrifugal action and air-volume control. All you have to decide is what type of pump will do the best job, at the least cost, and with adequate dependability. This is not a monumental feat; I will make it simple, and, perhaps, even fun. Just think of the satisfaction you will have when your neighbors inquire about your new irrigation system and you can spout off facts and figures about pumping water that will amaze them. Following is a step-by-step look at the types of pumps to consider.

Effluent Pumps

These are the least expensive pumps — selling for under $100 — and are very dependable. General-purpose pumps, they are sometimes called sump pumps or utility pumps. Don't let the fact that they are often called sump pumps confuse you.

When most people think of a sump pump, they envision a pedestal pump that sits in the corner of a basement and removes unwanted groundwater. Pedestal sump pumps can be used for light irrigation, but typically they create problems and don't have a long life expectancy when used routinely for pumping the necessary volume of water to irrigate even small lawns and gardens.

Pedestal pumps attract some buyers because they are inexpensive (usually under $60), but beware: You get what you pay for. Pedestal sump pumps are okay for occasionally pumping a sump in a wet basement, but they are not suitable as an irrigation pump.

Submersible effluent pumps, on the other hand, can handle the demands of average home irrigation needs and more. These pumps are more expensive, but not much more, and they are far superior in dependability and longevity.

The convenience of submersible effluent pumps is that typically they are equipped with a standard, plug-in cord so you don't need to hard wire an electrical system. The downside is that for irrigation purposes, using the pump requires plugging it in and then unplugging it when the watering is complete. This is a bit of a hassle, but relatively simple.

An effluent pump is designed to pump water that does not contain large solids. In other words, effluent pumps should not be used to pump household sewage, but they can be used to pump any type of water. The most common use of effluent pumps is for pumping gray water (waste water that doesn't contain sewage) from plumbing fixtures, such as washing machines, sinks, and bathing units, to gravity-drop drainpipes.

Effluent pumps also are used to control water in wet basements, and to pump water out of pools, ponds, and similar vessels. For irrigation purposes, effluent pumps are very effective in pumping water from cisterns, sumps, and other types of shallow water sources.

Many effluent pumps have 2-inch discharge outlets. A 2-inch pipe can deliver a lot of water to an irrigation system. Other models have 1½-inch outlets or 1¼-inch outlets. Any of these sizes is more than adequate for irrigation purposes.

There are several basic terms to be aware of to make a smart buying decision: voltage, horsepower, cable length, and floats.

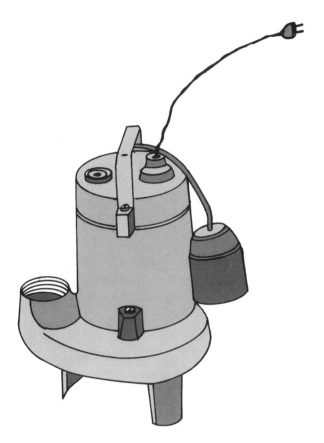

A submersible effluent (sump) pump is an affordable and convenient way to meet average home irrigation needs. It doesn't require any special wiring and is very effective for pumping from a variety of shallow water sources.

Voltage Requirements

Voltage is pretty simple to figure out on your irrigation pump. Some pumps require 230 volts, but they are larger than what most homeowners will want for irrigating their properties. A pump with a voltage rating of 115 volts should be adequate, and it is more compatible with average household electrical circuits. Make sure the voltage of any pump you choose is compatible with your household wiring. This is not usually a problem with an effluent pump, but it's important to double-check.

SELECTING AND INSTALLING A PUMP

Horsepower

The horsepower of an effluent pump is important; it affects the height and volume of water that is pumped in a given time. For example, a pump with a ¼-horsepower motor will pump water about 20 feet above the pump location, at a rate of about 38 gallons per minute (gpm). In contrast, the same type of pump with a ⅓-horsepower motor will pump water about 28 feet above the pump, at a rate of about 50 gallons per minute. A ½-horsepower pump produces about 60 gallons of water a minute at a height of about 35 feet.

Horsepower plays a vital role in the performance of a pump. Fortunately, simple irrigation systems do not require extensive water pressure or gallons per minute, which means that you can have a satisfactory system with minimal cost.

When you evaluate your pump needs for irrigation purposes, the most important factor to consider is how high the water must be pumped, determined by how deep your well is, and the ground elevation of the area you're watering. Once you know this, you are ready to assess the performance curves of various pumps to see if they meet your needs. Any reputable pump dealer will be happy to provide you with performance curve charts on available pumps. The chart will show the number of gallons per minute and the height water can be lifted by a specific pump model.

Cable Length

The length of the electrical cable on an effluent pump limits the depth of water in which it will work. Most of these pumps have either a 10- or 15-foot cable length, which has a direct bearing on how deep the pump can be submersed in water. If you plan to install the pump at greater depths you should consider a jet pump.

Floats

Floats on effluent pumps work quite simply. When the float has risen to a certain point, the pump comes on; when the float drops back down to a certain point, the pump cuts off. This system works well for most uses of effluent pumps, but is not the most effective for pumping irrigation water, since you don't want continuous pump operation.

There are three basic types of floats used on effluent pumps. One type is an integral part of the pump housing and normally gives the best service. It also minimizes damage to the float and prevents foreign objects from jamming the float.

Internal floats are the most dependable type of float to use with an effluent pump. With any type of float in operation, you normally have to deal with the inconvenience of plugging and unplugging the pump, but the low cost of the pump offsets this inconvenience somewhat.

The second best type of float is one that moves up and down on a guide attached to the exterior of the pump casing. These floats can become stuck, but generally they are very dependable.

The third type of float is placed on extension arms or connected to the discharge pipe. These tend to get stuck on the sides of sumps. While arm-floats and wire-floats work well most of the time, they are likely to cause more trouble than other types of floats.

Conclusions on Effluent Pumps

In the simplest terms, an effluent pump is an excellent choice (efficient and affordable) when you have a shallow water source (no deeper than 8 to 12 feet) and are not intimidated by having to spend time plugging and unplugging the pump.

Single-Pipe Jet Pumps

A single-pipe jet pump, also called a shallow-well jet pump, normally is used to pump water into a home from a shallow well with a depth of less than 25 feet.

Jet pumps are not submersible; normally they are installed in basements, pump houses, or similar locations, and can be mounted on a pressure tank. These pumps are capable of producing a dependable flow of water at heights of less than 25 feet.

Single-pipe jet pumps are pretty much automatic and require little effort on the user's part. Once properly installed, a jet pump takes over, which is a big time advantage over an effluent pump.

Single-pipe jet pumps retail for between $300 and $400. Additionally, in order for jet pumps to work efficiently and survive for an extended period, a pressure tank and related fittings are required. These cost about $200. The total cost will thus be between $500 and $600.

A jet pump can be used without a reserve pressure tank, but the pump will run longer than necessary, resulting in an early burn-out of the pump. For all practical purposes, you must plan on a complete installation package when installing a jet pump.

Why Pay So Much More?

There are two primary reasons for buying a jet pump instead of an effluent pump. If the depth of a water source is more than 14 feet, an effluent pump is not feasible. When the height of the pump lift (or the depth of the well) ranges from 15 to 25 feet, a single-pipe jet pump is the most logical choice.

The convenience of a jet pump is another advantage over an effluent pump. A jet pump is hard-wired and automatic, so there is no cord to plug and unplug. There are other advantages.

Effluent pumps produce water at a fairly constant, nonadjustable pressure. Jet pumps, on the other hand, allow regulation of the pressure point. In the case of sprinkler systems, and similar irrigation systems, this feature is very desirable.

Horsepower

Should you choose to pull your irrigation water from a pond, stream, or well with a depth of up to 25 feet, a single-pipe jet pump is a wise decision. Let's look for a moment at the technical stats on single-pipe jet pumps.

A jet pump with a ⅓-horsepower motor will lift water 25 feet at a rate of 345 gallons per hour (gph) at 30 pounds of pressure. When the pressure is increased to 40 pounds per square inch (psi), the volume drops to 120 gph. If the pressure is reduced to 20 psi, the output is 345 gph, the same as at 30 psi. If the water is only being lifted 15 feet, the output at 20 psi or 30 psi is 600 gph. At 40 psi the volume will be 360 gph.

Increasing the horsepower rating of the pump to ½ horsepower makes a big difference at 40 psi. For example, at 20 psi or 30 psi the output is 395 gph. At 40 psi, the volume of water produced reaches 280 gph, which is more than double the output of a pump with a ⅓-horsepower motor. The greater the horsepower rating, the more volume of water pumped at equal depths and pressures.

Dual-Pipe Jet Pumps

Dual-pipe jet pumps are designed for use with wells deeper than 25 feet. These deep-well pumps require two pipes; one to push water and the other to suck it up to the pump.

Dual-pipe jet pumps cost about the same as single-pipe jet pumps. The additional pipe and material required to install a deep-well jet pump adds to the cost, however.

Dual-pipe jet pumps are not as efficient as deep-well submersible pumps (see following section). While jet pumps are less expensive than submersible pumps, the value may not be as good in the long run. Dual-pipe jet pumps are capable of pumping from depths of 120 feet, which is much deeper than their shallow-well cousins can go, but not nearly as deep as deep-well submersible pumps can reach.

Dual-pipe jet pumps in the same basic price range as shallow-well pumps will lift water about 70 feet. At this depth, a ⅓-horsepower pump will produce 200 gph. A ½-horsepower pump will produce 300 gph.

If the water level to be pumped is deeper than what a standard dual-pipe jet pump can handle, you can opt for a multistage pump. These pumps are still jet pumps, but they can pull water up from depths of 160 feet. Multistage pumps cost considerably more than standard jet pumps (between $700 and $925).

When a well is deep enough to require more than a single-pipe pump, submersible pumps are usually the best choice.

Submersible Deep-Well Pumps

Submersible deep-well pumps are the best option for pumping water that is deep in the earth. They are normally used for wells 40 to 500 feet deep. Unlike jet pumps, submersible pumps are suspended below the water surface inside the well.

The price of an average submersible pump ranges from about $500 to $700. This is, of course, more than the cost of a jet pump, but submersible pumps give better performance and less trouble.

When you get into submersible pumps, you can have more water than you know what to do with if your water source replenishes itself quickly. For example, you can pull 120 gallons of water per minute (gpm) from a depth of 300 feet with a submersible pump. If you want more performance, you can get it with a larger motor or a high-flow pump.

Uses and Benefits

Unless you are going to drill a special well just for your irrigation needs, you probably will not need a deep-well pump. Even if you are planning a separate well for irrigation purposes, it is unlikely the well will have to be deeper than what a shallow-well pump will handle.

Having a deep well drilled and installing a submersible pump is expensive. The well will probably cost between $1,000 and $1,800. When you add the cost of a pump, pressure tank, and related installation equipment, your total cost could easily hit $2,500 or more. This kind of expense is justified only to serious irrigation enthusiasts.

Combining Pump Duties

An alternative to installing independent pumping systems for irrigation work is to use your existing well and water pump and keep your costs to a minimum. Combining pump duties for household and irrigation use is often possible for average home lawn and garden needs. There are, however, a few factors to weigh before making the decision to force your existing well and water pump into double duty.

What Is Your Well's Water Reserve?

You can determine your well's water reserve, or how much water is available in your well at any given time, by performing a simple test.

Take a piece of jute cord, or some similar string, and tie a small weight to the end — an old bolt or even a kitchen fork will do. The length of the cord depends on the depth of your well; it should be a little longer than what you believe the depth of the well to be.

Remove the cover from your well and lower the weighted end of the string into it until the weight hits bottom and the string begins to develop slack. Retrieve the string.

As you pull the string out of the well you will notice a point where the string is wet. Mark the wet spot with a marker or a knot. Pull the remainder of the cord out of the well and lay it on the ground. Measure the length

of the cord from the weight to the mark where you first found water. This simple procedure will tell you the depth of your water reserve.

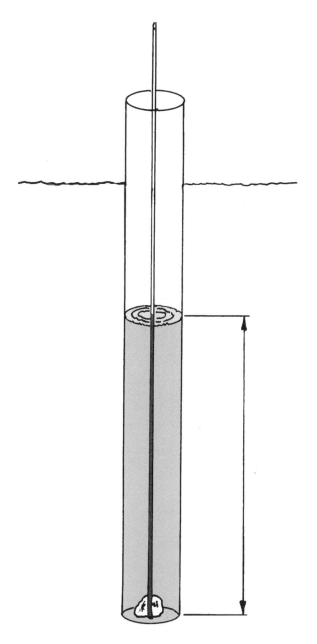

To determine how much water is available in your well at a given time (the reserve), tie a small weight to the end of a piece of cord and drop it to the bottom of the well. Once you've pulled it up, measure the length of string that is wet.

SELECTING AND INSTALLING A PUMP

Once you know this, measure the diameter of the well. Drilled wells have diameters of about four inches and dug wells will be about three feet wide. From these two measurements, a pump dealer can calculate the number of gallons of water available in the well. For example, a shallow well with a diameter of 3 feet and a water reserve of 7 feet contains approximately 371 gallons of water.

What Is Your Well's Recovery Rate?

If you have a dug well, the recovery rate probably will not be known. Drilled wells, however, are measured for recovery rates at the time of drilling. If you have the paperwork from your well installation, it may indicate the recovery rate.

If you can't find any documentation on the recovery rate of your well, you can figure out some average numbers. Most residential wells have recovery rates of at least 3 to 5 gpm. Some wells don't produce as much water, and others have recovery rates much higher. Planning on a rate of 3 to 5 gpm is probably safe. If you want to know precisely, call a professional plumber or a well expert to measure the recovery rate for you.

What Is Your Pump's Flow Rate?

A pump's flow rate is rated in gallons per minute (gpm). If you are going to be tapping into an existing well and pump system, this information is not too critical. However, if you are planning to install a second pump in your existing well to water your grounds, you need to make sure the pump you install doesn't produce at a gpm rate higher than the well's recovery rate.

If you have a well with a recovery rate of 3 gpm and you install a pump with a flow rate of 5 gpm, you will have a problem. The pump will be capable of pumping water faster than the well can produce it, which will result in a well that is pumped dry.

Combination

Knowing your well's reserve and its recovery rate, and your pump's flow rate, will give you a good starting point to determine if your well is capable of providing adequate water for irrigation and domestic use. It is wise, however, to consult with a local professional, once you have these basic facts, to make certain the well can pull double duty.

Once you are satisfied that your well is strong enough to provide the volume of water needed, you must decide how to combine your irrigation system with your domestic water system. There are two basic options. In some cases, you can install a separate pump system for the irrigation work and use the existing well. A less expensive and easier alternative is to tap into the existing well piping or water distribution pipes for your irrigation supply. When the quantity and frequency of irrigation water demand is moderate, as it is with most home gardens and lawns, tapping into the existing plumbing system makes a lot of sense and saves a lot of money.

Installing A Second Pump

Installing a second pump for an existing well is not a huge job. Most handy homeowners can accomplish the task in one weekend. The cost for this type of work, however, can be substantial, and there are times when it doesn't make sense.

If you have a deep well equipped with a submersible pump, it is not feasible to install a second pump for the well. The diameter of a drilled well is too small to accommodate two pumps safely.

Normally a shallow well has a large diameter and can accept the suction pipes from several pumps. In some cases it makes sense to install a separate pump system for irrigation when a shallow well is the water source, but the process is still more expensive than tapping into the existing pump system. Unless there is some functional reason why the existing pump cannot be tapped into, such as location and proximity to the site to be irrigated, tapping is the most economical solution.

Chapter 9 provides detailed technical information for making connections, adding second pumps, and a variety of other aspects of installations.

Tapping Into an Existing System

Tapping into an existing well system is not complicated or expensive. It is a job any mechanically inclined individual can do in less than a day, and the cost for the tap-in will be under $20. This cost doesn't include the piping and fittings used in the irrigation system, but it covers all the items used in the actual tap-in.

When you compare a tap-in, at a cost of $20, to the installation of a pump system, at rates ranging from just under $500 to over $1,000, it doesn't take long to see the advantages of tapping into an existing system.

There are many ways to make the connection between an irrigation system and an existing pump system, but the most common is in the pump house, basement, or crawl space, whichever is applicable to the specific job. This makes accessibility reasonably good and keeps strenuous work to a minimum.

Depending on the type of pipe used in the existing system, the tap-in can be completed in less than an hour by someone with a little experience in do-it-yourself projects. A professional can do it in less than 15 minutes.

With all factors considered, tapping into an existing system is the most economical way to get your irrigation water. As long as your existing well and pump are capable of producing the water you want, and any good pump dealer or plumber will be able to advise you on this issue, you can't beat the low cost and convenience of the tap-in method.

Installing a New Pump System

If you are going to drill a new well for irrigating your property, you will need to install a new pump system. This is not as difficult as many people believe.

Single-Pipe Jet Pumps

A single-pipe jet pump works on a suction principal. The pump sucks the water up the pipe and into the home. With a perfect vacuum at sea level, a shallow well pump may be able to lift water to 30 feet. This maximum

SELECTING AND INSTALLING A PUMP

lift is not recommended and is rarely achieved. If you need to lift water higher than 25 feet, investigate other types of pumps. If you can use a shallow-well jet pump, begin by asking a pump dealer to size your pump.

A Step-by-Step Guide to Installation

The single pipe from the well to the pump usually has a diameter of 1¼ inches. A standard well pipe material is polyethylene, rated for 160 psi. Begin by making sure the single suction pipe is not kinked or coiled. If the pipe holds an air pocket, priming the pump can be quite difficult. In most cases a foot valve will be installed on the end of the pipe to be submerged in the well.

Installing the pipe in the well. Screw a male insert adapter into the foot valve. Place two stainless steel clamps over the well pipe and slide the insert fitting into the pipe. Tighten the clamps to secure the pipe to the insert fitting.

Lower the pipe and foot valve into the well, but don't let the foot valve sit on the bottom of the well. If the suction pipe is too close to the bottom of the well, it may suck sand, sediment, or gravel into the foot valve, preventing the pipe from pulling water from the well.

When the pipe reaches the upper portion of the well, make a 90-degree turn in the pipe with an insert-type elbow in order to exit the well casing. Always use two clamps to hold the pipe to its fittings. When the pipe leaves the well, it should be buried underground, deep enough so that it will not freeze in the winter. This depth will vary from state to state. Your local plumbing inspector will be able to tell you how deep to bury the water supply pipe.

Burying the pipe. Dig a trench that is approximately 1 foot wide and below the frostline. Place the pipe in the trench, being careful not to lay it on sharp rocks or other objects

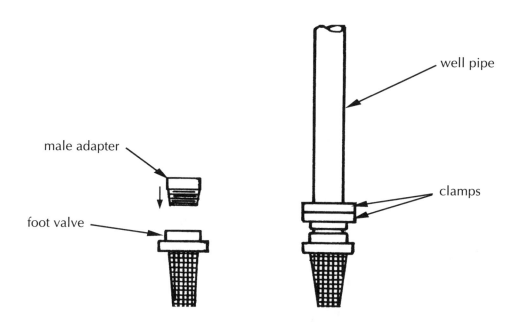

Installation of a jet pump begins with the foot valve. Screw a male adapter into the valve, and then secure the well pipe to the foot valve with two stainless steel clamps.

WATERING SYSTEMS FOR LAWN AND GARDEN

Trench-Digging Tips

- Check with utility companies to ensure that you will not damage underground utilities during your digging.

- Use a spade to cut through existing turf.

- Remove sod and place it on a plastic sheet or tarp.

- Don't mix dirt and sod together during the digging process.

- Keep dirt on one side of trench and sod on the opposite side.

- For large jobs, consider renting a trenching machine.

- Create a solid base within the trench for installation of the pipe.

- Make certain no sharp objects,

- like jagged rocks, will damage piping once installed.

- Install piping so that it lays flat and is not kinked.

- Backfill the trench slowly, don't just dump heavy loads of dirt on the pipe; damage to the piping may occur.

- Avoid backfilling with rocks or other sharp or heavy objects that might damage the piping.

- Compact the layers of backfill material as they are installed, to prevent settling and depressions in your ground at a later date (this can be done with a rented tamper or homemade tamper consisting of two pieces of wood nailed together to form a T shape).

that might wear a hole in it. Backfill the trench with clean fill dirt. If you dump rocks and cluttered fill on the pipe, it can be crimped or cut. To bring the pipe into your home, run it through a sleeve where it comes through or under the foundation. The sleeve should be two pipe sizes larger than the water supply pipe.

Connecting to the pump. Once inside the pump house, or wherever your pump will be located, the water supply pipe should run directly to the pump. The foot valve acts as a strainer and as a check valve. When you have a foot valve in the well, there is no need for a check valve at the pump.

Attach your incoming pipe to the pump at the inlet opening with a male adapter. At the outlet opening, install a short nipple and a tee fitting. At the top of the tee, install reducing bushings and a pressure gauge.

From the center outlet of the tee, your pipe will run to another tee fitting. Install a gate valve in this section of pipe, near the pump. At the next tee, pipe the center outlet to a

SELECTING AND INSTALLING A PUMP

pressure tank. From the end outlet of the tee, your pipe will run to yet another tee fitting. At this tee, the center outlet will become the main pipe for your irrigation system. On the end outlet of the tee, install a pressure-relief valve. All of these tee fittings should be in close proximity to the pressure tank.

Wiring. Your pump will be equipped with a control box that requires electrical wiring. This job should be done only by a licensed electrician.

Priming. The pump has a removable plug in its top to allow for priming. Remove the plug and pour water into the priming hole. Continue this process until water is standing in the pump and visible at the hole. Apply pipe dope to the plug and screw it back into the pump. When you turn the pump on, you should have water pressure. If you don't, continue the priming process until the pump is pumping water. This can be a time-consuming process; don't give up.

Pressure Setting. Once the pump is pumping water, the pressure tank will fill. When the tank is filled, your pressure gauge should read between 40 and 60 psi. The pump's controls will be preset at cut-in and cut-out intervals. These settings regulate when the pump cuts on and off. Typically, a pump will cut on when the tank pressure drops below 20 pounds. The pump will cut off when the tank pressure reaches 40 pounds.

If you prefer higher water pressure, the pressure switch can be altered. You might have the controls set to cut on at 40 pounds and off at 60 pounds. These settings are adjusted inside the pressure switch, around electrical wires. There is possible danger of electrocution when making these adjustments. Unless you are experienced with such work, leave the adjustments to a licensed plumber or electrician.

The adjustments are made by turning a nut that sits on top of a spring in the control box. If you attempt this, and I don't recommend that you do, cut off the power to the pressure switch before opening it. You will see a coiled spring, compressed with a retaining nut. By moving this nut up and down the threaded shaft, you can alter your cut-in and cut-out intervals.

CAUTION: The voltage from the wires in the pressure switch can deliver a fatal shock. Do not attempt this job unless you are experienced in such work.

Dual-Pipe Jet Pumps

Dual-pipe jet pumps, also known as deep-well jet pumps, are needed when your water level is more than 25 feet below the pump. A dual-pipe pump or a submersible pump are your options for this deep a well. Submersible pumps normally are used in deep wells. However, dual-pipe jet pumps also will get the job done.

Dual-pipe jet pumps look similar to single-pipe pumps, are installed above ground, and are piped in a manner similar to them as well. The noticeable difference is the number of pipes going into the well.

The operating principals of the two types of pumps differ. Single-pipe (shallow-well) jet pumps suck water up from the well.

WATERING SYSTEMS FOR LAWN AND GARDEN

Dual-pipe (deep-well) jet pumps push water down one pipe and suck water up the other.

Installation

The only major installation differences between a single-pipe jet pump and a dual-pipe jet pump are the number of pipes used in the installation, and the use of a pressure control valve. Dual-pipe jet pumps use a foot valve and have a jet-body assembly that is submerged in the well and attached to both pipes and the foot valve. The pressure pipe connects to the jet body first, and the foot valve hangs below this pipe. There is a molded fitting on the jet body for connecting the suction line. The jet body allows both pipes to connect in a natural and efficient manner.

Dual-pipe jet pumps push pressure down the pressure pipe with water pushed through the jet-body assembly, and makes it possible for the suction pipe to pull water up from the deep well. From the suction pipe, water is brought into the pump and distributed to the potable water system. When you look at the head of a dual-pipe jet pump, you will see two openings: The larger one is for the suction pipe, the smaller opening for the pressure

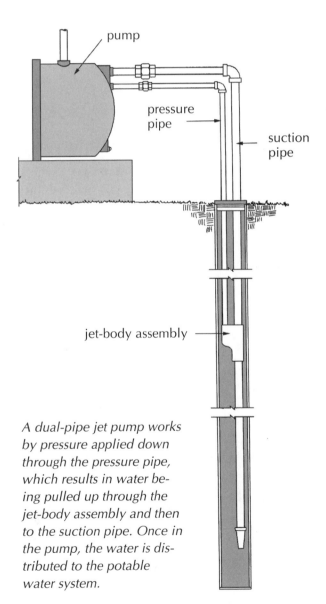

A dual-pipe jet pump works by pressure applied down through the pressure pipe, which results in water being pulled up through the jet-body assembly and then to the suction pipe. Once in the pump, the water is distributed to the potable water system.

Detail of dual-pipe installation at ground level.

SELECTING AND INSTALLING A PUMP

pipe. The suction pipe usually has a diameter of 1¼ inches. The pressure pipe typically has a diameter of 1 inch.

The piping from the pump to the pressure tank needs a pressure-control valve to ensure a minimum operating pressure for the jet-body assembly. Single-pipe pumps do not require a pressure-control valve. Once the pressure control valve is installed, the remainder of the piping is done in the same manner as used for a single-pipe pump.

Submersible Pumps

Submersible pumps are very different from jet pumps. Jet pumps are installed outside of the well. Submersible pumps are installed in the well, submerged in the water. Jet pumps use suction pipes. Submersible pumps have only one pipe and they push the water up the pipe, from the well. Jet pumps use a foot valve, submersible pumps don't. Submersible pumps are much more efficient than jet pumps; they

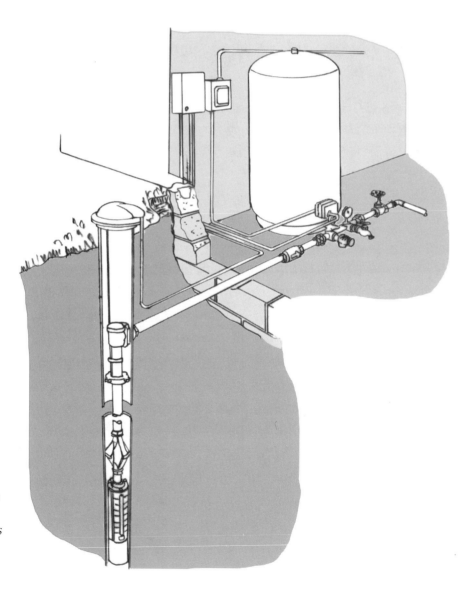

A submersible pump is installed inside the well, submerged in water. The water is then pushed up from within the well. This pump is more efficient than a jet pump.

WATERING SYSTEMS FOR LAWN AND GARDEN

also are easier to install. Under the same conditions, a ½-horsepower submersible pump can produce nearly 300 gallons more water per minute than a ½-horsepower jet pump. With so many advantages, it is almost foolish to use a jet pump, when you could use a submersible pump.

Installation

Installing a submersible pump requires techniques different from those required for a jet pump. Since submersible pumps are installed in the well, electrical wires must be run down the well to the pump. Before installing your submersible pump, consult a licensed electrician about the wiring needs of your pump.

Installing the pitless adapter. You will need a hole in the well casing to install a pitless adapter to provide a watertight seal for your well pipe to feed your water service. When you purchase your pitless adapter, it should be packaged with instructions on the size hole you will need in the well casing.

You can cut a hole in the well casing with a cutting torch or a hole saw. The pitless adapter attaches to the well casing and seals the hole. On the inside of the well casing, you will have a tee fitting on the pitless adapter, which is where your well pipe is attached. This tee fitting is designed to allow you to make all of your pump and pipe connections above ground. After all the connections are made, lower the pump and pipe into the well, and the tee fitting slides into a groove on the pitless adapter.

Installing the pipe. To make the pump and pipe connections, you will need to know the depth of the well. The well driller should provide you with the depth and rate of recovery for the well. Once you know the depth, cut a piece of plastic well pipe to the desired length. The pump should hang at least 10 feet above the bottom of the well and at least 10 feet below the lowest expected water level.

Apply pipe dope to a male-insert adapter and screw it into the pump. This fitting is normally made of brass. Slide a torque arrestor over the end of your pipe. Next, slide two stainless steel clamps over the pipe. Place the pipe over the insert adapter and tighten the two clamps. Compress the torque arrestor to a size slightly smaller than the well casing and secure it to the pipe. The torque arrestor absorbs thrust and vibrations from the pump and helps to keep the pump centered in the casing.

Slide torque stops down the pipe from the opposite end of the pump. Space the torque stops at routine intervals along the pipe to prevent the pipe and wires from scraping against the casing during operation. Secure the electrical wiring to the well pipe at regular intervals to eliminate slack in the wires. Apply pipe dope to a brass, male-insert adapter and screw it into the bottom of the tee fitting for the pitless adapter. Slide two stainless steel clamps over the open end of the pipe and push the pipe onto the insert adapter. After tightening the clamps, you are ready to lower the pump into the well.

Installing the pump in the well. Before lowering the pump, it is a good idea to tie a safety rope onto it. After the pump is installed, this rope is tied to the top of the casing to prevent the pump from being lost in the well, in case the pipe becomes disconnected from the pump. Next, screw a piece of pipe or an adapter into the top of the tee fitting for the pitless adapter. Most plumbers use a rigid piece of steel pipe for this purpose.

Once you have a pipe extending up from the top of the tee fitting, lower the whole assembly into the well casing. This job is easier if you have someone to help you. Be careful not to scrape the electrical wires on the well casing as the pump is lowered. If the insulation on the wires is damaged, the pump may not work.

Holding the assembly by the pipe extending from the top of the pitless tee, guide the pitless adapter into the groove of the adapter in the well casing. When the adapter is in the groove, push it down to fit into the mounting bracket. This concludes the well part of the installation.

Connecting the Water Distribution System. Attach your water service pipe to the pitless adapter on the outside of the casing. You can do this with a male-insert adapter. Once inside the pump house, the water pipe should have a union installed in it. The next fitting should be a gate valve, followed by a check valve. From the check valve, your pipe should run to a tank tee.

The tank tee is a device that screws into the pressure tank and allows the installation of all related parts. The switch box, pressure gauge, and boiler drain can all be installed on the tank tee. When the pipe gets to the tank tee, the water is dispersed to the pressure tank, the drain valve, and the water main. When the water main leaves the tank tee, you should install a tee to accommodate a pressure relief valve. After this tee, you can install a gate valve and continue piping to the water distribution system. The only task left is to test your system; you do not have to prime a submersible pump.

Alternative Water Sources

I mentioned alternative water sources earlier in this chapter. People who pay for their water by the gallon or who don't have wells capable of handling the demands for domestic use and irrigation, often seek alternative water sources. We already have looked at most types of water sources in previous chapters, but let's take a little time to see how to get that water to your lawn or garden.

Unless you have a massive area to irrigate you probably will not want to make the cash investment required to drill a well and install an independent pump system. This makes sense and is certainly understandable. A driven well, a stream, a pond, or even a catch basin can overcome the high cost of drilling a well for modest irrigation needs. The problem is, how do you get the water to where you want it?

With any of the less expensive water sources, a jet pump should be more than capable of getting the job done. Effluent pumps will perform well in many instances, and there will almost never be a need for a deep-well pump. This is all good news economically.

Depending upon your creativity, you may be able to water your garden without the use of a pump. This saves money on the cost of equipment and on the cost of electricity, plus it is more environmentally responsible. We are going to explore this possibility in the next chapter.

It has been my experience that effluent pumps and jet pumps are the only two types of pumps generally needed for residential irrigation. I have told you about deep-well pumps to inform you and to be fair to you, even though I doubt that you will have to install one. It is, however, very likely that you will work with deep-well pumps if you elect to use the tap-in method of connection.

The simplicity and low cost of effluent pumps and single-pipe jet pumps makes setting up a home irrigation system a breeze. Given the proper circumstances, you can avoid high water bills and still enjoy a lush lawn and a green garden.

~ ~ ~ ~ ~

OVERVIEW OF PUMPS

Type	Advantages	Disadvantages
Effluent Pump	Inexpensive Very dependable General purpose Standard plug-in — require no special wiring Suitable for simple household irrigation needs Effective for pumping water from cisterns, sumps, and other shallow water sources	Requires plugging to start and unplugging to stop For shallow wells only — not suitable for wells deeper than 12 feet Constant, nonadjustable water pressure
Single-Pipe Jet Pump (also called Shallow-Well Jet Pump)	Automatic — does not require turning on and off Good for wells 15 to 25 feet deep Adjustable water pressure	Shallow wells only — no deeper than 25 feet Not submersible 3 to 4 times more expensive than effluent pump Requires hard wiring
Dual-Pipe Jet Pump (also called Deep-Well Jet Pump)	Good for wells deeper than 25 feet — pumps from depths of 120 feet	Not as efficient as deep-well submersible pump
Submersible Deep-Well Pump	Better performance, more dependable than jet pump Pumps from depths of 500 feet Plentiful water — pulls up to 120 gpm from depth of 300 feet	More expensive than dual-pipe jet pump Expensive to install Requires separate well

SELECTING AND INSTALLING A PUMP

~ 6 ~

Moving Water by Gravity Distribution

THE GREAT THINGS ABOUT GRAVITY distribution in an irrigation system are its simplicity and its low operating cost. There is no need for either electricity or a pump. Not all irrigation situations can be handled by a gravity system, but many small gardens can be watered easily without the use of expensive equipment and electricity.

In the context of this chapter, gravity distribution applies to any way of getting irrigation water into the soil of a garden or lawn without the use of a pump. Some of the examples I mention occasionally require a pump, but the day-to-day irrigation work is done with the use of gravity flow. If you can use one of these systems, you can save considerable energy costs.

Example 1: Watering a Vegetable Garden

To start, assume that you live in a rural location and enjoy planting a vegetable garden each year. The garden plot measures roughly 30 feet x 40 feet. This is not a huge garden, but it is large enough to make watering a bit of a chore. You want to find a way to reduce your watering responsibilities and the time spent tending to them.

Your garden is on fairly flat ground, and there are no natural water sources close by. You receive your drinking water from a shallow well, but you don't feel the quantity of water is adequate to use for irrigating your crops. How are you going to design an inexpensive watering system?

The first problem to solve is to find a source of water. You don't want to go to the expense of drilling a well and installing a pump, so you must look for some other alternative. After weighing all of your options, you decide to buy an aboveground swimming pool to use as a cistern. The pool will be placed near the garden and filled periodically with water from your well. The cistern will catch rainwater and store it. By adding to the natural water supply in the pool on a gradual basis, you can maintain a satisfactory water level without putting a strain on your well.

Now that you have a source of water, you have to decide how to distribute it throughout your garden. There are various ways to go about the distribution.

Slotted-Pipe System

A slotted-pipe system is an inexpensive way to distribute water from your cistern to the garden. The only requirement is to have a tap or drain near the bottom of the swimming pool. Since the pool and the garden are situated on land of approximately even topography, you will have to rely on the pressure of the water in the pool to push the liquid out and through the piping system. This is such a simple, yet effective, way to water a weekend vegetable garden.

Building a Slotted-Pipe System

Start by establishing your water source. In our example, the water source is a pool, with a drain valve installed near the bottom. The drain valve empties into the top of a solid pipe connected to a system of slotted pipes. When the drain valve is opened, water drains into the solid pipe and flows to the various branches of slotted pipe. The slotted pipe can be laid out on top of the ground or installed beneath the surface.

If the pipe is installed below grade, it should be surrounded by crushed stone and, ideally, be covered with a filter fabric to keep the system from clogging. As the slotted pipe accepts a flow of water from the cistern, it disperses the water, through the slots in the pipe, to the roots of thirsty plants. This is a low-impact, inexpensive gravity system to build.

Laying out the pipe. If you recall, the garden in our example is 30 feet x 40 feet. This gives you two primary ways to lay out your slotted pipe. Typically, the pipe will be laid to run in the same direction as the garden rows. The amount of slotted pipe needed will depend on how the pipe is routed and the amount of coverage you desire. It is best to run a length of pipe in each row of the garden, but it can be run with some other piping scheme, such as one pipe in every other row. This reduces the area covered by irrigation water, but it also reduces your costs. However, slotted pipe is not very expensive, so you won't have to sell your house just to buy some extra pipe.

Installing the pipe. The type of slotted pipe used for this system is sold in large rolls and is the same type used as perimeter drains around houses. For that use, the solid portion of the pipe rests on the earth with the slots facing upward. Run-off water enters the slots and is then carried away from the foundation of the home.

When used for irrigation purposes, the pipe can be installed upside down with the solid part of the pipe on top and the slots on the bottom. Some people prefer to install the pipe with the slots facing upward and the far end of the pipe capped off. In this position, the pipe collects water until it is full, then any excess water entering the pipe is forced out through the slots on the top. Either method works.

Aboveground installation. If you install your slotted-pipe system on top of the ground, take some precautions against wind or other disturbances that may move it. One of the easiest ways to secure your pipe is to drive gutter spikes through the top of the pipe

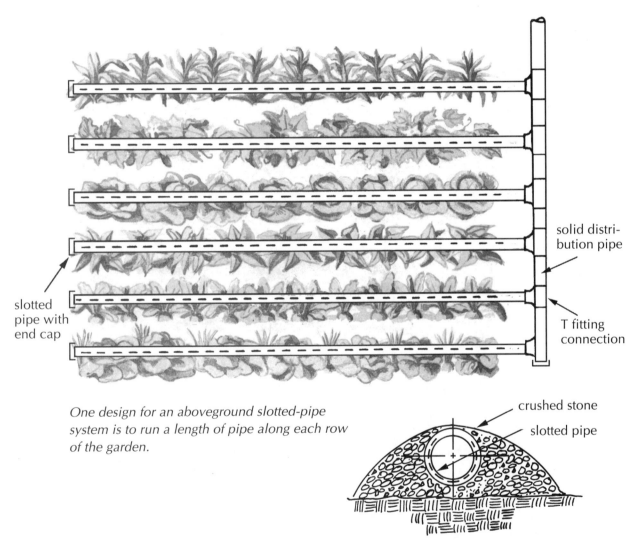

slotted pipe with end cap

solid distribution pipe

T fitting connection

One design for an aboveground slotted-pipe system is to run a length of pipe along each row of the garden.

crushed stone

slotted pipe

If aboveground slotted pipe is installed below grade, it should be surrounded with crushed stone and covered with a filter fabric to prevent clogging.

MOVING WATER BY GRAVITY DISTRIBUTION

and into the ground. These spikes look like big nails and will pierce the plastic, slotted pipe with ease.

Other methods can be employed to hold the pipe in place, but I've found that gutter spikes work well. Any type of U-shaped bracket can be placed over the pipe to hold it in place. The key is to secure your drainage system so that it will not require your frequent attention.

Slotted pipe is generally thin-walled, making it susceptible to collapse if it is stepped on or run over with a piece of equipment. As long as you are aware of this, it should not pose any serious problems. The advantage of this lightweight pipe is that it is easy to move around. You can remove a section for tilling and replace it in a matter of minutes. It also is no problem to remove the entire piping system in preparation for winter.

Belowground installation. If you don't like the idea of having black pipe laying around in your garden, you can install the pipe below grade. In doing this, it is important to mark all pipe locations. Unless you bury the pipe at a depth sufficient to protect it from a plow and tiller, you may find yourself repairing sections of it frequently.

To bury slotted pipe properly, first dig a trench to the desired depth. Fill the bottom of the trench with crushed stone. Lay piping in the trench and cover it with more crushed stone. The stone acts as a filter to reduce the likelihood of the slots in the pipe filling up with sediment. As added insurance, you can purchase pipe covered with factory-installed filter fabric.

So far, I've been talking about pipe that is corrugated, slotted, flexible, and sold in large rolls. This type works fine for garden irrigation,

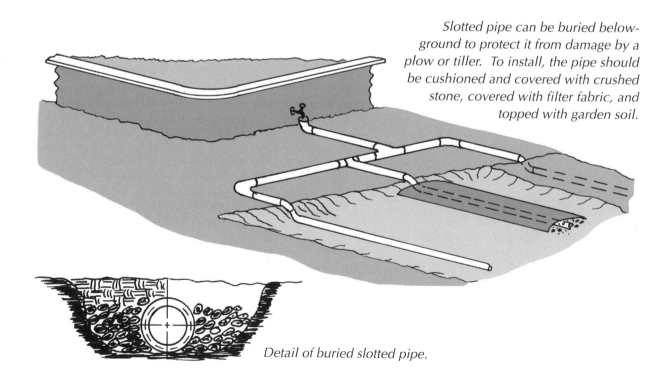

Slotted pipe can be buried belowground to protect it from damage by a plow or tiller. To install, the pipe should be cushioned and covered with crushed stone, covered with filter fabric, and topped with garden soil.

Detail of buried slotted pipe.

WATERING SYSTEMS FOR LAWN AND GARDEN

and is inexpensive. If, however, you prefer working with rigid pipe, you can use the type of slotted pipe that is used in drain fields for septic systems. You should still bed the pipe in stone and cover it with a layer of stone.

Either type of slotted pipe is easy to install. You don't have to be a master plumber to make the connections, and both types of pipe are light enough in weight to make them comfortable to work with alone. The only tool required is some type of saw to cut the pipe, such as a hacksaw, carpenter's saw, or most any other type of saw.

In-Ground Cistern

Returning to our example, assume that you don't want to install an aboveground cistern, and that your garden is less than 100 feet away from your home. You decide to construct a modest in-ground cistern by digging a hole lined with a waterproof tarp. Water will be distributed to your garden with a slotted-pipe, in-ground system. You only have two problems: How will you keep the cistern full? And, how will you get the water into the piping system?

Say that your house is equipped with gutters ending just above splash blocks. You also have a sump pump in your basement that pumps surface water out from under your basement floor during wet seasons. The discharge hose for the sump pump runs to a graveled dry well in your backyard.

With a little trenching, either by hand or with a walk-behind trencher, which can be rented by the day, you can connect your downspouts and sump pump discharge to an underground piping system that will convey the run-off water into the in-ground cistern. What a great way to manage water. Instead of wasting it, you're storing it for dry spells.

Setting Up the Connections

To create this type of underground drainage system, you will need some solid pipe, some fittings, a saw, and a means for making a trench. The size of your drainage pipe should be no less than a 2-inch diameter; a 3-inch diameter is a much better choice. Schedule-40 plastic pipe, like plumbers use in homes, is ideal for this application. It is relatively inexpensive and easy to work with.

Start by putting adapters on the ends of your downspouts. Rubber couplings that slide over the end of a piece of drainage pipe and over the end of a gutter make this part of the job a breeze. If your gutter has an offset, like an elbow fitting, on the end, remove the fitting. You want your coupling to attach to a vertical section of the downspout.

Since you will be conveying excess water to the cistern with the use of gravity, the drainage pipe must be pitched slightly downhill. A minimum pitch of ⅛ inch per foot should be used. If your home sits high enough above your cistern to allow it, a ¼ inch per foot in pitch is preferable.

Assume that your home has two downspouts, one at each end of your house. Depending upon how the gutters were installed, there may be a downspout on each corner. In any event, start with the downspout farthest away from the cistern.

Use a wye fitting and an elbow fitting to connect the first downspout to the first section of underground drainage pipe. Run the underground piping along a path that will carry it near any additional downspouts. Connect every downspout to the underground piping in the same way. There are other fittings available with different angles of turns that can be used to ensure that everything comes together properly.

Once all the downspouts are connected to the underground drainage, begin to install drainage pipe leading to the cistern. Use another wye fitting, some reducing fittings, and a rubber coupling to connect the discharge hose of the sump pump to the drainage system. When you get the drainage piping to the cistern, allow it to protrude over the opening, so that your cistern will collect water every time it rains or your sump pump cuts on.

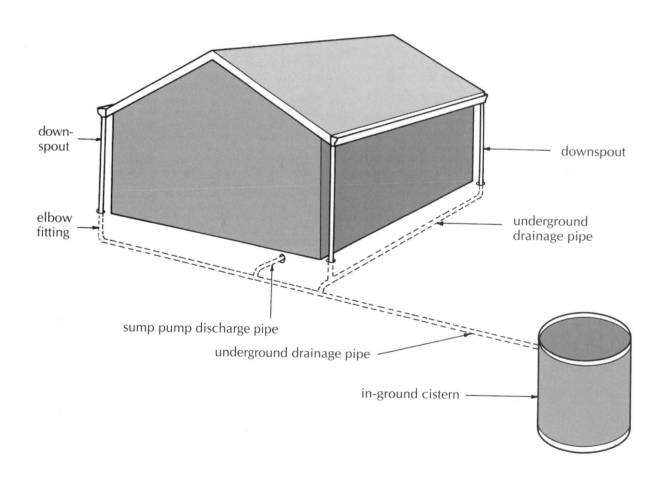

Rainfall run-off and sump pump discharge can be directed for irrigation purposes with an inexpensive system of underground drainage pipes running to a cistern. By pitching the drainage pipe slightly downhill, no power is needed to move the water into the cistern.

WATERING SYSTEMS FOR LAWN AND GARDEN

Watering the Garden

Now you have a water source, but how are you going to get the water into the garden? If your land is fairly level, you can't use the same procedure discussed with the aboveground cistern. If you aren't opposed to using electricity, you can set a submersible effluent pump in the cistern and run it off an extension cord from your home. This is a fast way to fill your irrigation pipes, and the amount of electricity used is minimal.

A hand-operated pump could be installed to allow water from the cistern to be pumped into the inlet pipe of the irrigation system. If you don't mind spending a little time and

Using Graywater for Home Landscape Irrigation

Residents of arid areas of the United States that suffer frequently from drought are looking to the water from showers, bathroom and kitchen sinks, bathtubs, dishwashers, and washing machines as sources for watering their home landscapes. While there are many legal restrictions on the use of this water, many of the Western states have started to ease these restrictions. Be sure to check your local ordinances before proceeding to use graywater.

Robert Kourik, author of *Gray Water: Use in the Landscape* (Santa Rosa, CA: Metamorphic Press), offers the following guidelines for the healthiest use of graywater.

~ Water in, water out. (Never store graywater, not even for a day. A properly-designed graywater system has a "surge" tank to temporarily hold the water until it's distributed.)

~ Your surge tank must have an automatic overflow pipe to the sewage line.

~ Never apply graywater with a sprinkler or onto a lawn.

~ Always plumb your system with valves so the graywater can be switched back to the sewer at any time.

~ Rotate the graywater throughout the landscape to avoid injuring plants.

~ Avoid soaps, detergents, and cleansers with boron, bleaches, and too much sodium. (Use liquid concentrates instead of powdered detergents.)

~ Flush accumulated salts deep into the soil once every three to five years in areas where it rains less than 15 inches per year.

~ 61 ~

effort in your watering program, you could dip 5-gallon buckets into the cistern and pour water into the distribution pipes. Of all the methods available, a submersible sump pump is probably the most feasible option.

Example 2: Lawn Watering

The underground drainage system discussed above for a garden can be used for a lawn as well. If you have a sump pump or rain gutters, why not harness the water and put it to good use? The method used to divert rainwater into your lawn is a little different than the one described for a vegetable garden, but the principal is similar.

For a lawn, you're not going to plow and till the soil, so the underground piping doesn't have to be buried as deeply as for a garden. In fact, it only needs to be deep enough to allow grass to take root over it. Also, the distribution piping in a lawn can have a much

smaller diameter, so as not to create a series of 4-inch-wide trenches.

Suppose your front lawn has a slight incline sloping down to the road in front of your home. Since this is the lawn that everyone sees, it is most important to keep it green. To accomplish this, install a loop irrigation system, which consists primarily of one large-diameter supply pipe (about 3 inches in diameter) and a network of numerous ¾-inch distribution pipes.

Building a Simple Lawn Watering System

The design of this system is simple. The first step is to direct the gutter downspouts and the discharge hose of your sump pump connect to a common 3-inch, underground pipe, as described in the cistern example on page 59. Instead of running the end of your drainage pipe to a cistern, run it in front of your house. The drainage pipe should be in

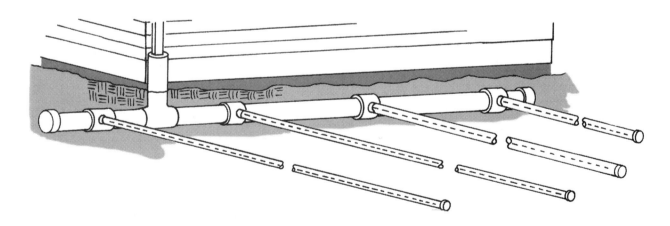

A simple lawn-watering system can be constructed with a network of underground perforated pipes that receive runoff from your house's downspouts. The water is distributed solely by gravity.

Pipe Options

There are three types of plastic water pipe you may use in your distribution system: polybutylene pipe (PB), polyethylene pipe (PE), and PVC pipe.

PB pipe is my first choice for almost all water requirements. Like PE pipe, PB pipe is sold in rolls, but can be purchased in rigid lengths. The pipe is gray and very durable. It is possible to kink PB pipe, but it takes a lot of effort to do so. Accidental kinking is uncommon. Like PE pipe, barbed insert fittings are used to make joints with PB pipe. Compression joints can be used, but insert fittings and crimp rings make a more secure connection. The result is an instant joint. I've used PB pipe for years in my contracting business, and to this day I've never had a leaky joint. I wholeheartedly recommend PB pipe.

PE pipe is a good choice for underground irrigation. This black pipe comes in a flexible roll, and joints are made with barbed insert fittings and hose clamps and require no curing time. This pipe is available in a number of sizes, but you will most likely use ¾ inch, 1 inch, and 1¼ inch.

There are a few drawbacks to working with PE pipe. If not handled properly, the pipe tends to kink up. Even if the kink is straightened out, the wall of the pipe is weakened by the stress. Sharp stones can cut through the pipe if they are allowed to rub against it, such as when a riding lawn mower is passing over the buried pipe. If pockets of water are left in the pipe during winter months, the piping may split from pressure created by ice within the pipe. All in all, PE pipe is a good choice, but there is a better one.

PVC pipe is the least suited to irrigation applications because it is rigid and becomes very brittle in cold weather. The process of making joints with PVC pipe is simple on the surface, but a bit more complicated in the field. The joints are solvent welded (glued) together. Both the ends of the pipe and the hubs of the fittings must be clean and dry, which can be a problem when installing the pipe below grade. A cleaner/primer must be applied to the pipe ends and the fitting hubs prior to making a joint.

stalled parallel to the front of your home. Cap off the end of the pipe.

Tee fittings. As you install the pipe in your front yard, install tee fittings at regular intervals, based on the width of your yard. The fittings should be installed so that the tee outlets are in a horizontal position, facing into the slope of your lawn. The most appropriate fittings have 3-inch openings on each end and a 1½-inch opening at the tee outlet. This 1½-inch opening will be reduced to a ¾-inch diameter with female adapters.

Female adapters are installed in the following manner: Place a glue-together joint between the tee outlet and the hub of the female adapter, providing you have a 1½-inch threaded opening and allowing the use of threaded reducing bushing to make the opening smaller. You will end up with an opening equipped with ¾-inch female threads. These outlets will accept male adapters.

Installation

Screw ¾-inch male adapters into the waiting outlets along the main underground drain. These create a proper connection point for whatever type of plastic water pipe you use.

Building the distribution network. Connect your first distribution pipe to a male adapter. Dig a trench so you can run the pipe underground through your lawn, perpendicular to your home. In this example, it should run down the incline and toward the road. Continue this process until you have as many feeder lines running through the lawn as you want. Cap off the end of each feeder line.

Perforate the pipe. The next step is to drill holes along the tops of the pipes. The bigger the holes, the better. If you are willing to take the time, drill holes in the top and both sides of the pipe.

Filling the trenches. After you have created your perforated pipe, backfill the narrow trenches with small, rounded stones, which will act as a filtering agent. Obviously, the stones need to be larger than the holes you have drilled in the pipes. Now you can backfill the trenches and replace the sod strips. Your system is installed and ready to work. Every time it rains, your lawn will get a nice even distribution of water.

There is an added bonus with this type of system. Not only will it water your lawn effortlessly, you can use the network of piping to distribute plant food or growth stimulators. Just loosen one of the rubber couplings from a downspout, pour in the plant food, and flush it out into the system with your garden hose. The result will be a healthier lawn.

A Trickle System

A trickle system (also called a drip system) can be an excellent way to meet irrigation needs. Sophisticated commercial trickle systems are expensive, but you can create your own homemade version inexpensively. Assume that your water source is a cistern located close to your garden, and equipped with a drain near the bottom fitted with standard hose threads, like those found on boiler drains and outside faucets.

Make the Most of the Rainfall in Your Garden

One simple way of maximizing the effect of each rainfall you receive is to dam the rows of your garden. This involves creating miniature dams at both ends of every row to trap rainwater as it falls. Depending upon the soil conditions, row dams can provide a few extra days of water to your crops. In terms of cost, all that is required is a small amount of work with a shovel.

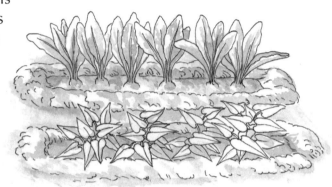

Gardens on steep inclines will not enjoy the same benefits from row dams as gardens on level ground, since the natural slope of the land will force water to the low ends of the rows. There is, however, a way to beat this problem, and, again, the cost is negligible.

If you cut into the side of the hill where the garden will be planted, rows can be stair-stepped down the side of the hill. This might be done with a shovel and hoe, or a small bulldozer or backhoe, depending on the size of the garden and the consistency of the ground.

Once the garden rows have been stepped down the hill, looking like wide steps, they're ready for planting. This design slows down running water from the top of the hill, reducing erosion and providing additional water to the rows. Also, since the rows now have a flat exposure to the sky, they will catch more rain as it falls. Terraced gardens are very effective in hilly terrain.

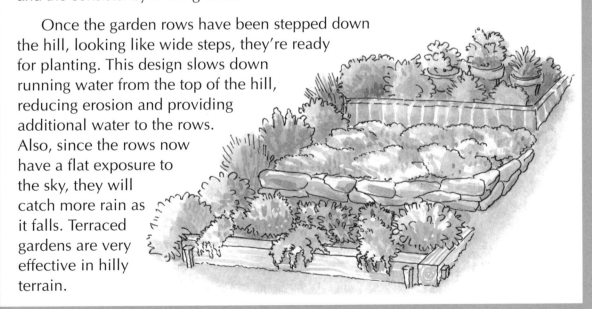

System Design

A trickle system begins with a connection such as a garden hose, attached to the drain of the cistern. You need a male connector for the opposite end of the hose, and a female connector on the end of your main trickle pipe. These adapters/connectors are sold in most hardware stores and other stores catering to lawn and garden enthusiasts. They typically come with a barbed insert on the end opposite the female connector. To install these, place a clamp over the end of a flexible pipe and push the barbed insert into the end of the pipe. Slide the clamp into place, so that it is resting over the barbed section, and tighten. Now you have your main trickle pipe adapter connected to a hose and mated to the cistern.

The type of pipe used in the trickle system is not critical, but some types are better than others. The piping doesn't have to be large — an inside diameter of either ⅜ inch or ½ inch

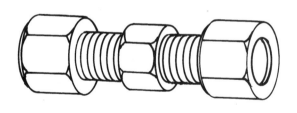

Compression fitting

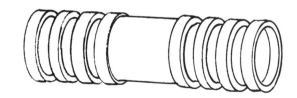

Barbed fitting

will do fine. My personal favorite is ½-inch polybutylene pipe (PB), which is easy to work with and will not damage easily. Polyethylene (PE) pipe is black and draws heat. If the pipe is laying on top of the ground during a hot day, it can become quite soft and stepping on the pipe or running over it with a wheelbarrow full of weeds can damage it. This won't happen with PB pipe, which is tougher.

Rigid pipe sections can be used in a trickle system, but I prefer coils of PB pipe. A 100-foot coil of PB pipe costs less than $25. Once the pipe is uncoiled and laid out straight, it is easy to manipulate. It can bend around turns, run over humps, and wind through a corn field in a serpentine method. Since PB pipe retains its shape so well, there is never a problem picking it up and relocating it. PE pipe can get so flimsy that rough handling can crimp it, and rigid pipe is difficult to move around in long sections. I believe PB pipe is the best material for the job.

Installing the Pipes

How you install your trickle system will depend on the layout of your garden. Assume the crops are planted in rows that run away from the cistern. This is the easiest type of layout to work with; keep this in mind when positioning your cistern.

The main trickle pipe connected to the cistern should be one pipe size larger than the feeder pipes. For example, ½-inch feeder pipes require a main pipe with a diameter of ¾ inch; ⅜-inch feeder pipes need a ½-inch main pipe. To work with PB pipe, you only need caps, several tee fittings, crimp rings, and a crimping tool. If you don't want to go to the bother of renting a crimping tool, you can buy compression fittings to use with the PB pipe.

Commercial Drip Systems

If you prefer to use commercially available drip irrigation equipment, you will find a wide choice of emitters, minisprays, and misters available. A drip or trickle system is especially useful where you have special plantings that are unevenly spaced or require deep or special watering.

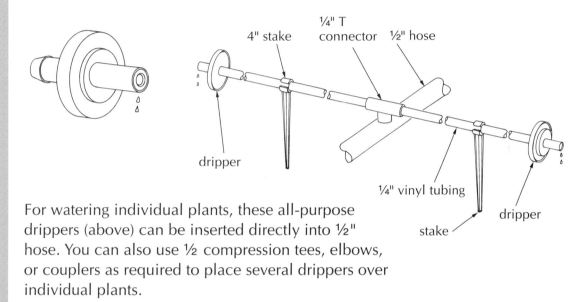

For watering individual plants, these all-purpose drippers (above) can be inserted directly into ½" hose. You can also use ½ compression tees, elbows, or couplers as required to place several drippers over individual plants.

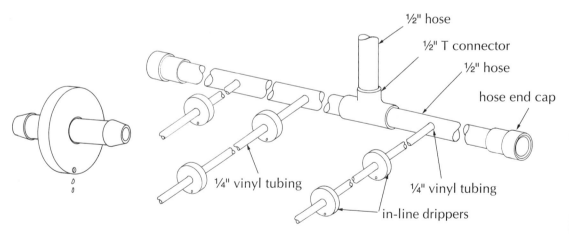

For watering multiple vegetable plants in rows (not more than 15' long), small in-line drippers work well. These fit into ¼" vinyl tubing that runs directly from ½" hose.

MOVING WATER BY GRAVITY DISTRIBUTION

While these fittings are not as dependable when the pipe is under considerable pressure, such as providing water in your home, they will work well with this low-pressure installation.

Compression fittings are easy to use, and the only tools needed to make the connections are two adjustable wrenches or a couple of pairs of pliers. To make a compression connection, first remove the compression nut, revealing a thin, round ferrule on the inside. Without a ferrule, a compression fitting will not work. Slide the compression nut over the end of a piece of pipe. Follow the nut with the ferrule. Push the end of the pipe into the compression fitting. When the pipe is into the fitting fully, slide the ferrule and nut up to the fitting. Turn the nut clockwise to tighten it. Make sure the pipe doesn't slip out of the fit-

ting while you are working. As the nut tightens, it compresses the ferrule, creating a watertight joint. There's really nothing in this job to intimidate you.

Building the System

Begin by installing a tee fitting with the hose from the cistern connected to the tee outlet and sections of your main trickle line

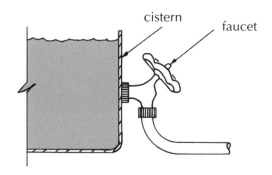

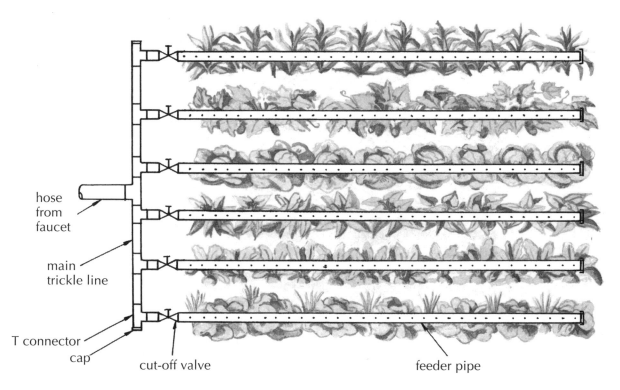

You can make your own trickle (or drip) system with feeder pipes that run down every row of your garden.

WATERING SYSTEMS FOR LAWN AND GARDEN

(the largest one) connected to each end of the fitting. Your goal is to run the main trickle line perpendicular to the rows in your garden. With this first tee installed, you are ready to extend the sections of the main line.

Installing the main line. As you install the main line, think ahead. You need to install a tee in the main line to line up with each row in your garden. The tee fittings will be the same size on each end as the main pipe, with the tee outlet being sized to fit your feeder pipes. This installation can be buried, but an aboveground system is easy to move around and is not as prone to clogging. Once you have the main pipe running the width of your garden, cap off each end of it.

Connecting the feeder pipes. For the sake of convenience, say that your rows are fifty feet in length. Cutting a roll of PB pipe in half provides two fifty-foot lengths of pipe. You can cut PB pipe with most any type saw, but a fine-tooth hacksaw works very well. Special cutters are made for working with PB pipe, but they are expensive and not necessary.

Drilling holes. Cut lengths of pipe to run the length of your rows. Lay the pipe out and let it relax into a natural, straight shape. At some point, you have to drill holes in the feeder pipes. You can do this before or after they are connected, but you do have to do it. The size of the holes will vary with the size of the pipe, but they do not have to be large, as long as they have a diameter large enough to allow water to seep out.

Cap off pipe ends. Once you have connected the feeder pipes to the main trickle pipe, cap off the ends of the feeder pipes. With the flex- ibility and light weight of PB pipe, you can position your feeders close to your plants. If you need to weave your way around obstacles, the PB pipe is flexible enough to do so without using offset fittings. Now you are ready to water your garden.

When you open the boiler drain at the cistern, the distribution pipes will fill with water. As the pipes fill, water will begin to seep out of the trickle holes. Once you see how the water is flowing, you can begin to close the valve on the boiler drain until you achieve just the amount of flow you want. By having the water trickle out with a low flow rate, you give your plants the necessary water they can absorb without the waste of excess water running down the hill.

Adjusting the Flow

There may be some plants in your garden that require more water than others, but with the trickle system and a little advance planning, you can overcome this problem. When you plant your garden, plant the thirsty plants closest to the cistern. As you run the feeder pipes down the rows, you can install cut-off valves in the piping, which allows you to control the water flow, watering only the plants that need it. Not only does this maximize the growth potential of your plants, it conserves water. In fact, let's look at this a little closer.

Assume that the first five rows of your garden are planted with corn. The last two rows of your garden are planted with watermelons. The middle rows are planted with tomatoes, squash, lettuce, and so forth. Let's further assume that you want to provide more water for your watermelons than you do for your lettuce. By installing valves at each tee where the feeder pipes connect, you can cut off water flowing to any feeder pipe. If you choose to only water your melons, you can close off all the valves for every feeder pipe, except those serving the melons.

Maybe you will want to water in some alternating fashion. For example, you might water tomatoes on Monday, corn on Tuesday, and so on. This is easy. Just close the valves on feeder pipes that you don't want in operation, and open the ones you do.

The trickle system we have just examined is very effective, and not particularly expensive. In our example we used a cistern as a water source, but you could just as easily connect the garden hose to an outside faucet on your home and do the watering with your household supply. One big advantage to a trickle system is that it doesn't waste water like a sprinkler system. With the mobility of PB pipe, you can keep all the water coming out of your feeder pipes right where it belongs, next to the vegetables. It is also possible to introduce plant food into the trickle system and have it distributed to your crops with the water. For a garden of modest dimensions, this is one of the best systems I've ever used.

Disadvantages of Gravity Distribution

Irrigating with only the power of gravity is not always feasible. If you are unwilling, or unable, to have a cistern or an elevated water tank, gravity irrigation is pretty difficult. A great deal depends on the topography of your landscape. Naturally sloping lawns offer more opportunity to use a gravity system. Likewise, the elevation of your garden in relation to the surrounding land is a deciding factor. In general, the size of an area that can be watered by a gravity system is restricted. Unless your irrigation area happens to be below a large water source, like a pond, lake, or river, you will not be able to use huge amounts of water.

A sensible cistern will not hold enough water to irrigate a large garden through a whole summer. Unless you are willing, and able, to supplement the water caught by your cistern, it is highly unlikely that you will enjoy a large enough quantity of water to get through the summer. For this reason, and others, most irrigation systems rely on pressurized water systems, as discussed in Chapters 7–10.

~ 7 ~

Surface and Overhead Irrigation for Lawns and Gardens

S URFACE AND OVERHEAD irrigation systems for lawns and gardens range from simple garden-hose sprinklers to elaborate piping systems. These irrigation methods typically depend on a pressurized water system for smooth operation. It is possible to design some systems to work on gravity distribution, but most require a higher degree of water pressure. The amount of pressure needed depends on the type of system. In general, normal household pressure will be more than adequate. The water pressure in most homes ranges from 40 pounds per square inch (psi) to 80 psi, with an average of 40 to 50 psi. Since so many of the systems discussed in this chap-

ter depend heavily on water pressure, I'll begin with that.

Water Pressure

Water pressure is a critical factor in the successful operation of most irrigation systems. Some systems need strong pressure to spray water into the irrigation area. Other systems require low pressure, so as not to waste water. When installing an irrigation system, first consider your need or desire to control the water pressure.

How can you control water pressure? The answer depends on the type of water supply you are using. Managing the water pressure of a municipal water service is different from adjusting the pressure created with a pump system.

Municipal Water Sources

When water is run from a city water main to a home, the water pressure can be extremely high. If the street pressure is in excess of 80 psi, a pressure-reducing valve is required within the foundation of the home. There are several good reasons why the plumbing code restricts the maximum allowable water pressure in residences.

A strong water pressure can be detrimental to a plumbing system and dangerous to the users of the system. Say, for example, the water pressure in your home was unregulated and reached surge peaks of 125 psi. When you turn on the kitchen faucet to fill a glass with water, such a strong water force might knock the glass out of your hand and break it in the sink, causing shards of glass to fly about. This is not just an example I made up — I've worked on plumbing systems where this has happened.

When the household water pressure is extremely high (above 80 psi), the strain on pipe joints and faucets can be more than they can handle. A strong water hammer with heavy pressure can cause pipe joints to break loose, flooding a home. Extreme pressure can deteriorate faucets to a point where they drip. There are many good reasons for limiting household pressure to 80 psi.

In a residential application, a pressure-reducing valve is not very big. It is installed in the main cold water pipe close to where the incoming water service meets the main interior water pipe and serves all of the domestic plumbing.

By loosening a nut and turning a threaded control on the valve, a plumber can adjust the water pressure within certain ranges. For example, I could install a pressure-reducing valve on a water pipe that had an incoming pressure of 95 psi and set the outgoing pressure (the water being used in the home) at 70 psi. The adjustment range varies with individual reducing valves, but there is usually a range of 50 psi available.

If you have basic plumbing skills, a pressure-reducing valve is easy to install and adjust. You may find a need for installing one as you progress with your irrigation system. If you do, refer to Chapter 9 for complete details on the installation and adjustment procedures.

Pumped Water Sources

If you are using a pump to get water to your irrigation system, adjusting the water pressure will be done differently. There are many types of pumps used to move water, and not all are set up to allow for adjusting the output pressure. On an effluent (sump) pump, the pressure cannot be throttled. You can, however, inspect the pump prior to buying it to determine how many gallons of water it pumps per minute. All effluent pumps are rated with a gallons-per-minute (gpm) output.

Jet pumps, shallow-well pumps, and submersible pumps (for potable water) are all designed to work with pressure switches and pressure gauges that can be adjusted.

Pressure switches for well pumps are typically preset at the factory with a cut-in and cut-out pressure rating. For example, the switch will make the pump cut on if the pressure drops to 20 psi, and cut off if the operating pressure reaches 40 PSI. For more pressure, you can install a pressure switch that cuts on at 30 psi and off at 50 psi. It is also possible to make adjustments inside the pressure switch to alter the preset pressures. This process is discussed in detail in Chapter 10.

Whether you are using a well pump or water from a city supply, there are ways to control the water pressure available to an irrigation system. Of course, if you're using a hose connected to an outside faucet, you can open and close the faucet until you achieve a pressure that works best with your sprinkler or other equipment.

Surface Irrigation

Surface irrigation refers to equipment installed at ground level, such as a standard lawn sprinkler, a drip system, or a porous hose. Surface irrigation is probably the most popular system of irrigating, although it varies with regions of the country. One exception might be the irrigation of lawns in upscale neighborhoods, which are often watered with underground irrigation equipment and pop-up sprinkler heads. But in the fields of professional farmers, you're likely to see examples of surface irrigation. Golf courses and athletic fields often are watered with surface-mounted equipment. Within the broad category of surface irrigation, there are quite a few options for equipment.

Overhead Irrigation

Overhead irrigation uses equipment that releases water from above ground level. These systems mimic natural rainfall. While many overhead irrigation systems might also be called surface irrigation equipment because the base of the equipment sits on the ground,

the term "overhead irrigation" is used in this book to refer to water being dispersed from several feet above ground level.

An overhead irrigation system might consist of a tall pole equipped with perforated arms extending out over an area to water it. Or it could consist of a framework of posts, lattice, and a maze of overhead piping that drops water from above onto the plants.

Overview of Usefulness

Both surface and overhead irrigation systems have their place, but their use is not always equal in comparable situations. For example, take a front lawn. Would you want a tall, octopus-like sprinkler sitting in your front yard for most of the summer? Would you like to have row after row of overhead piping installed above your front yard? I assume your answer to both of these questions is "no." I don't blame you. On the other hand, would you object to a small, unobtrusive sprinkler being placed on your front lawn? Maybe, but probably not. Suppose I told you that there is a sprinkler that can move itself around your front lawn, providing good water coverage, even when you're not home to attend to it, would you consider putting it in front of your house? A lot of people would.

Now, switch from your front lawn to your backyard vegetable garden. Do you have any problem having a series of pipes installed over your crops if the pipes will increase the yield of vegetables? I doubt it. Could you use a walking sprinkler in your garden? Of course not, because the plants would prohibit its motion.

When evaluating irrigation systems, consider how the systems will be used and their

Matching Irrigation Systems To Your Needs

For Lawns

~ Underground systems work well

~ Surface systems are simple, inexpensive, and effective

~ Overhead systems and drip systems are not practical

For Vegetable Gardens

~ Underground systems may interfere with plowing and tilling work

~ Overhead systems are very good

~ Drip systems ae extremely effective

~ Porous hoses can be used, but may result in wasted water usage

For Flower Gardens

~ Drip systems are great

~ Porous hoses work very well

~ Underground sprinklers work well, but are expensive

~ Overhead systems detract from the beauty of the garden

For Individual Plants and Trees

~ Drip systems are best for watering "scattered" plantings

purpose. Overhead systems are rarely acceptable for use in watering lawns. Surface units don't work well for watering a garden because the water isn't high enough off the ground to reach all of the crops. While it's not definitive that surface units only work for lawns and overhead systems only work for gardens, it does tend to be so.

When I think of gardens, I usually think of vegetable gardens, but flower gardens are extremely popular, although they don't offer the same irrigation challenges as vegetable gardens. If you're growing roses or low-to-the-ground flowers, you can use a surface irrigation system. A flower that stands a foot high has considerably different watering requirements than a corn stalk over six feet tall. Fruit trees require a far different approach to irrigation than a plot of blueberries. There are many different types of gardens, and each has individual irrigation needs. For this reason, I can't lay out definitive guidelines to follow. You must assess the needs of each garden and lawn individually.

System Mobility

Mobility is one factor in considering an irrigation system. Do you want a system that can be put out in the morning and taken in by the afternoon, or do you want a system that is semipermanent in its placement? Few people will want a surface or overhead irrigation system for their lawn that is not easily removed. Gardeners may feel a bit differently. If you plant a garden in the same spot each year, there is probably no reason to be concerned about a semipermanent installation. As long as you can work your soil without interference from the irrigation system, there is no real need for removing it more

WATERING SYSTEMS FOR LAWN AND GARDEN

than once a year, if that often. Lawns, however, are a different story.

Anyone who is interested in a no-hassle approach to lawn watering, without creating an eyesore, is almost sure to use an underground sprinkler system. I just can't imagine having a lawn regularly cluttered with irrigation equipment. It's one thing to have a hose and a sprinkler on the grass for an hour or so in the morning, but leaving the rig in place all summer is unthinkable.

Mobility refers to more than just the ability to move irrigation equipment out of view; it also refers to how much area can be irrigated with a particular system. For example, a common sprinkler and garden hose is a very mobile, versatile irrigation device. It can be moved around a lawn at will, allowing full coverage, and then can be set in the backyard garden after the lawn has been watered. In contrast, an overhead system for a garden is not mobile and is limited to watering only the surrounding area.

All surface irrigation systems offer mobility to some degree, but not fully. Big irrigation sprinklers involve quite a bit of work to relocate. Large overhead sprinklers that *can* be moved, generally have to be towed with a truck or a tractor. This is not the kind of equipment you move casually every few hours to extend your irrigation range, a fact to consider before purchase.

Except with simple irrigation methods, mobility is usually limited. Obviously, standing in your lawn with a spray nozzle on your garden hose does not present much of a mobility problem, and neither does an inexpensive lawn sprinkler. When you step up to the next level, to serious irrigation systems, mobility becomes more of a factor. Many systems are not intended for frequent movement.

Some irrigation equipment is designed to stay in its assigned location for the entire season. Then there are units that can be rolled around with reasonable mobility, but not with enough ease to make the move enjoyable. Once you get beyond the needs of a watering can or garden hose, mobility becomes an issue to consider in selecting a system.

Appearance

The physical appearance of an overhead irrigation system can be attractive or ugly, depending on how much time and money you are willing to invest. If you live in the country, like I do, the appearance of your irrigation system may have little meaning to you. On the other hand, if you live in a subdivision and don't want your neighbors complaining about the looks of your irrigation system, you may have to spend considerable amounts of money to camouflage the piping.

Hiding the piping of an overhead irrigation system is not difficult, but it isn't cheap either. If exposed piping is likely to create problems for you, it may be more logical to irrigate with some type of mobile surface equipment. Consider this before you buy anything.

I have developed a fairly simple method of concealing overhead piping. I designed this out of necessity, when living in an area with some overly curious neighbors who made negative comments regularly about activities in the neighborhood. Even growing a garden caused a stir. When I built an overhead irrigation system, one of these neighbors became quite upset by its appearance, and compared it to outdoor plumbing and primitive living conditions. There were no rules or laws stating that I couldn't do what I had done, but the neighbor was persistent enough that I got tired of listening to him.

I thought about moving, just to get away from this outspoken neighbor, but moving was not a practical option. Instead, I came up with a way to conceal my overhead piping that was beautiful — it might even have made the cover of a gardening magazine!

Here's what I did. I began by putting 4-inch x 4-inch pressure-treated wooden posts into the ground at each corner of the garden. The overhead piping was already secured to an overhead rack. I installed vertical posts for the piping inside the wooden posts so that all of the piping and the rack were contained. I then nailed pressure-treated lattice to the posts and rack, both above and below the piping. The only pipe left in plain view was the main feed pipe running up the side of one of the wooden posts. I secured this pipe tightly to the post.

Finally, I camouflaged the entire structure with morning glories, ivy, and other climbing and clinging plants. It made an outstanding trellis that covered my vegetable garden and concealed all of my irrigation piping. Oh, and my neighbor actually complimented me on how nice the project turned out! I moved about two years later.

Equipment

Surface irrigation equipment is where most people begin their education in irrigation principals and practices. The first piece of equipment acquired is usually a basic garden-hose sprinkler, or perhaps it's a perforated water hose. In either case, most people don't start out with a high-tech watering system, because they don't have the need. The basic equipment is often all that is needed to receive desired results.

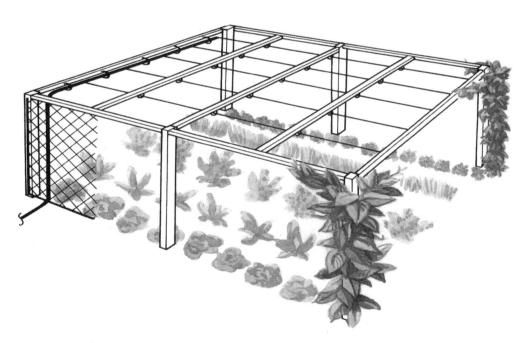

A wooden-frame overhead irrigation system doesn't have to be an eyesore. Try camouflaging the frame by growing climbing vines and other clinging plants along the posts. Latticework can be added on the sides to complete the "trellis" look.

WATERING SYSTEMS FOR LAWN AND GARDEN

Low-Cost Lawn-Watering Devices

Low-cost lawn-watering devices are very common. They are, in fact, probably the most popular type of home irrigation equipment. A rotating sprinkler is sometimes the only watering device needed for small-scale irrigation. Everyone has seen these sprinklers, and as kids, many of us used to play in their streams on hot days. As basic as they are, garden-hose sprinklers can be effective irrigation tools when properly matched to the job at hand. They are inexpensive, easy to move, simple to connect, and they can spray a substantial amount of water.

Garden-hose sprinklers come in different shapes and sizes. Some twirl around and others roll back and forth in an arc. There are also hose-type sprinklers that pulse water out in a stream. Quality and cost for these little irrigation devices are as varied as the sprinklers themselves. While this type of sprinkler is limited in features and benefits, it can accomplish a number of small watering jobs.

For example, a small flower or vegetable garden, 10 feet by 20 feet, could easily be maintained with a hose-type sprinkler. The question is, what type of sprinkler design will work best in this garden? If you use a twirling sprinkler, water will be wasted, because as the sprinkler turns and the water pressure is set high enough to reach each length of the garden, it will overshoot the width by 5 feet. Since there is no point in wasting water, you

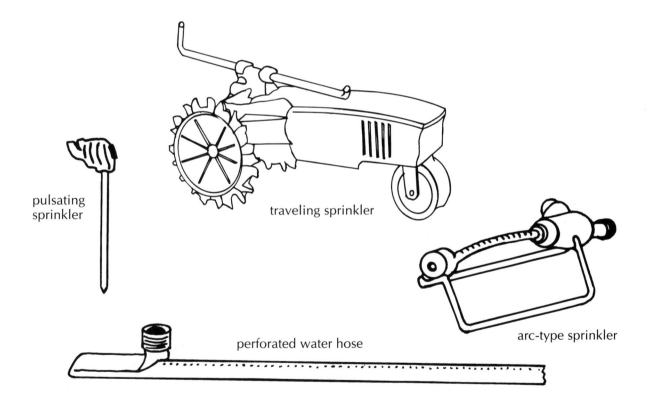

pulsating sprinkler

traveling sprinkler

arc-type sprinkler

perforated water hose

Sprinkler and other watering devices that attach to an ordinary garden hose come in a variety of models, depending on the size and needs of the area you are watering. You can set up a system connecting various sprinkler heads to meet the needs of each area of your garden or landscape.

SURFACE AND OVERHEAD IRRIGATION

Sprinkler Arc and Saturation Patterns

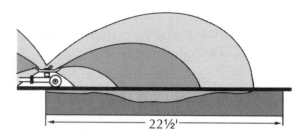

Plastic soakers, arc-type sprinklers, and sprinklers with revolving arms result in this erratic soakage.

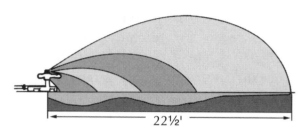

Oscillating, pulsating, or rotating sprinklers drop water unevenly, requiring overlapping sprays.

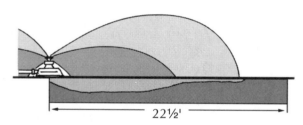

Whirling and fixed heads drop most of the water on the inside, requiring successive overlaps to obtain continuous coverage.

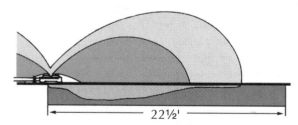

A cone spray soaks only a small area and needs to be moved often to be effective.

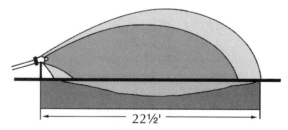

A slit-type sprinkler head throws most of the water 7 to 14 feet from its base.

should look at another style of sprinkler for such a garden.

A pulsating model that sticks into the ground and shoots a stream of water for some distance is an option. Most models rotate to some degree, but usually not in a full circle. This type of sprinkler would work well in a rectangular garden, but there are still other inexpensive options to consider.

An arc-type sprinkler may be the best design for a small, rectangular garden. By placing this type of sprinkler in the center of the plot, water could reach each end without spilling too much out of the boundary lines. Also, the arc-type sprinkler may have an advantage over the pulsating sprinkler, because a rolling arc of water produces a more uniform watering pattern, which is more desirable.

There is yet another option that could be the best overall choice for a little garden: a perforated water hose. This is a flat hose with tiny holes in it through which water sprays. By controlling the flow of water to the hose, you can adjust the range of the water spray. If the water pressure is turned up, rising streams of water will come out of the hose and fall back to the earth, watering it. Cutting back the hose pressure will result in more of a trickle system, which can be very effective for irrigation, and for conserving water.

WATERING SYSTEMS FOR LAWN AND GARDEN

Depending on the layout of the plants in the garden, it might be highly effective to use multiple perforated hoses. For example, if the garden contains three long rows of tomato plants, laying two perforated hoses on either side of the center row would provide excellent water coverage. A wye adapter could be used to connect both of the hoses to a single outdoor faucet. This type of design would be hard to beat. An alternative to hose watering is drip watering. Drip systems allow a user to pinpoint the location of water being dispersed. This not only conserves water, it ensures that the root structures of plants receive the water they need.

As you can see from this example, some irrigation devices work better than others, depending on the circumstances.

Bigger Equipment

If your surface irrigation needs require bigger equipment, there is plenty from which to choose. Perhaps one of the most versatile pieces is a unit containing irrigation hoses on a large drum. These units are mounted on a frame equipped with wheels, for easy moving. This type of equipment comes in various sizes to accommodate a variety of watering needs.

If you have a large lawn or large acreage, you may need larger equipment. A drum-mounted hose is useful for moving sprinklers around such an area.

SURFACE AND OVERHEAD IRRIGATION

These models use a standard hose connection. Operating water pressure ranges from 30 psi to 50 psi, depending upon the desired gpm. This pressure range is suitable for all standard residential water systems. Other features may include a two-wheel chassis for making mobility of the unit simple and easy, an automatic shutdown for the water motor, and selective automatic shutdown for the sprinkler. Various types of sprinkler heads can be used, and stabilizer feet keep the watering device stable. Hose guides assure proper hose packing, and a pressure gauge reads the inlet pressure of water serving the machine.

Mobile irrigation equipment, like the type just described, can be extremely versatile. At a flow rate of 4 gpm and an inlet water pressure of 33 psi, it is possible to produce a wet diameter of 82 feet. With a 70 percent efficiency rating, the irrigated area will be 58 feet by 250 feet — approximately ⅓ acre. A full acre can be given a 1-inch precipitation rate in just five days.

If you increase to 10 gallons of flow per minute and an inlet pressure of 66 psi, the area covered can be 77 feet by 258 feet. At this production rate, the machine irrigates nearly half an acre a day. A 1-inch soaking of three acres can be achieved in five days. This type of equipment is large enough to handle most residential irrigation needs, yet small enough to be manageable.

When you want more coverage, you can step up to a larger unit. These units can provide a wet diameter of 152 feet. The irrigation area is 106 feet by 213 feet. Over half an acre can be covered in a single day. To irrigate eight acres with a 1-inch rate of water takes five days. This coverage requires a 1-inch water connection and water pressure ranging from 45 psi to 87 psi.

Accessories are available for mobile irrigation systems. For example, a tall riser can be used to get the sprinkler head up high. This can be useful when watering corn or fruit trees. When you weigh the options of mobility, convenience, and performance, this type of roll-about irrigation system might be ideal for your lawn or garden.

Kid's Stuff

Irrigation needs are as different as the people who have them. While one person may be happy with a perforated hose and another a roll-around irrigator, some people prefer the simple pleasure of using kid's stuff to water their plants — there are some interesting items in the local toy store.

I bought my daughter, Afton, a water game consisting of a 5-foot plastic tower with a ball tied to it by a piece of string. To play, a hose is connected to the tower, the water is turned on and sprays out of the tower in two places, at the top and about mid-way up. Players stand in the spraying water and bat the ball back and forth with paddles.

This tower toy makes a dandy sprinkler for a small garden and is designed to spray water in a full circle from two heights — 2 feet above the ground, and about 5 feet above the ground. There is no bulky base to the plastic pole, it just sticks in the ground allowing it to be placed anywhere in a garden without crushing low-growing plants. By adjusting the water pressure, the amount of water spraying in your garden can be controlled.

The key to choosing the best device for the job is proper planning. Since this book is intended for people interested in watering average, residential lawns and gardens, I have not included information on irrigation equipment manufactured for professional farmers or with other large-scale commercial applications in mind.

Building Overhead Irrigation Systems

How you construct an overhead irrigation system is up to you. You can use either rigid pipe or flexible tubing to create your waterway. You will need a support system, or wood to attach the piping. Pressure-treated lumber works well, but there are times when a pipe frame is better suited to the conditions. The framework is critical to a good overhead irrigation system.

A Pipe Frame

A pipe frame has some advantages over a wood frame: it is lighter weight, depending on the type of pipe used for the frame. Do you want to dismantle your irrigation system at the end of the growing season? You can do this with either a wood or pipe frame, but plastic pipe is much easier to maneuver than heavy, pressure-treated wood. If you are building a permanent structure, either material will do nicely.

Selecting Pipe

To build a pipe irrigation frame, I recommend using Schedule-40 plastic pipe and fittings. The pipe size is not critical, but 1½-inch pipe is easy to work with, inexpensive, and sturdy. I wouldn't recommend anything smaller. Building the frame with 2-inch pipe gives more strength to the frame, but the added strength is not needed as long as you

Overhead System Materials List

Support Posts	90-Degree Fittings
Outer Frame Material	45-Degree Fittings
	Couplings
Cross Structures	Tees
Piping	Glue, Solder,
Valves	Crimp Rings
Pipe Clamps	

Advantages of a Pipe Frame

~ Lightweight

~ Easy to work with

~ Inexpensive

~ Simple to dismantle

~ Easy to install year after year

~ Will not rot

~ Will not attract wood-infesting insects

Disadvantages of a Pipe Frame

~ May lack stability

~ Can warp in excessive heat

~ Does not present as many options for an attractive installation as does wood don't make long runs without vertical supports, and these will be needed with either size pipe.

The best Schedule-40 pipe is PVC pipe, which is the white plastic pipe used in homes for drains and vents. Another type of Schedule-40 pipe is black ABS pipe, but it doesn't work as well for this application. ABS is easier to cut than PVC, but either can be cut with a hacksaw or a standard carpenter's saw. PVC is generally less expensive than ABS.

The main reason I recommend PVC pipe is that it holds its shape better in hot conditions than does ABS. If a 20-foot length of ABS pipe is laid across a pipe rack on a truck during a hot day, the pipe will sag and develop a warped slope. PVC pipe doesn't do this. If you don't like the idea of having a white irrigation frame, you can always paint the PVC another color. But if you use ABS, don't be surprised to see your frame sagging in hot sunlight.

Building the Support Frame

To build the frame, you will need to dig a few holes deep enough so they are below the frost line. Then pour concrete into the

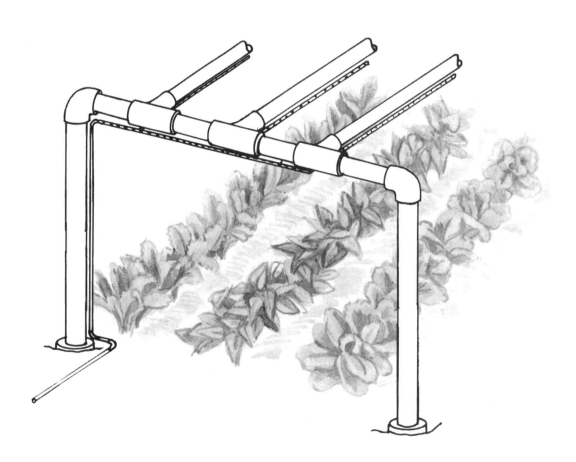

An overhead pipe frame is easy to make and to take down when the gardening season is over. The frame is constructed of Schedule-40 plastic pipe. PE pipe is attached to the frame to distribute water over each row of the garden.

WATERING SYSTEMS FOR LAWN AND GARDEN

holes to create a pier foundation, or, if you prefer, you can get by with just the holes for your support.

Dig a hole at each corner of the irrigation boundary. In addition, you need interim posts at 10-foot intervals to support the frame pipes. Schedule-40 pipe is available in 10-foot sections.

Set the vertical supports in the holes, keeping the tops of the supports level. Sloping or rolling topography makes this a little challenging. To level, run a string between two of the corner posts, place a string level on it, and adjust the depth for the two posts until the bubble is in the center of the level. Use the string as your guide while installing additional vertical supports between the two corners.

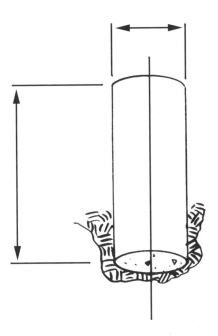

Concrete piers make a good foundation for a pipe frame. The holes need to be below the frost line to provide a permanent foundation that will last through the winter for use the next season.

Move the string to another corner post and continue this process until all of the installed support posts are level with each other.

If your land has a radical difference in topography, you can install a 10-foot section in one part of the garden, providing an 8-foot ceiling, and install a 12-foot section, for instance, at the low end to keep the frame level.

Installing Horizontal Pipes

Now that all of the vertical sections are in place, you are ready to create the frame. For a permanent installation, glue the fittings and pipe together. For a temporary framework, don't glue the joints. PVC pipe fits firmly into fittings, even without glue. If you glue the joints and later decide to relocate the frame, a few couplings will splice the work back together after cutting it for movement.

To create a frame you will need some Schedule-40 fittings: elbows, tees, and couplings. The tees will be used to connect the horizontal frame to vertical interim supports. Elbows or street ells (fittings where one end accepts pipe and the other end slides into the hub of a fitting) will be used in conjunction with the tees to shape the frame. There should be little need for couplings, since your interim supports are set to support the pipe at approximately 10-foot intervals.

The best way to make joints with PVC pipe is to use a primer and glue but using just glue will work also. Make certain that the hubs of fittings and ends of pipes are clean and dry, or the joints will be weak.

Place the tee outlets of the tee fittings on the vertical support pipes. Use elbows or street ells to make necessary turns in the framework. The width of your garden will determine the number of supports through

SURFACE AND OVERHEAD IRRIGATION

the middle of the garden plot. Tees can be installed with the tee outlets laid pointing down to accommodate this need. Once the frame has been made, you are ready to install your overhead piping.

The type of pipe used for dispersing water depends on your preference. Copper pipe works well, but is expensive and needs to be soldered to put it together. Or you can use compression fittings, which again, is costly.

CPVC pipe is joined with glue. Personally, I don't like working with CPVC, but some homeowners do. I prefer to use polybutylene (PB) pipe for the distribution system. I wouldn't recommend polyethylene pipe (PE), because it weakens in direct heat.

Secure the pipe to the frame with cable ties, which resemble the plastic ties often sold with disposable garbage bags. One end of the cable tie slides through the hole in the other end of the tie, and the ridged strip locks the tie in place. Cable ties are available in various lengths, and can be wrapped around the frame and water pipe at the points to be secured.

If you use rigid pipe for your water distribution, you will need numerous elbows and couplings; however, when rolls of PB pipe are used, there is little need for fittings. The PB pipe is flexible enough to turn and make offsets without using fittings. You still will need some couplings, however. To save yourself the expense of renting a crimping tool, you can buy compression couplings, which work admirably in this function.

Installation. The actual installation of distribution piping is simple, and there are numerous techniques that can be employed to give your irrigation system a personalized touch. For example, you could install an overhead distribution pipe above each garden row. If you want to save some money on pipe and use less water, you can install the piping between rows. You can even zig-zag piping across the frame to water your plants. How you lay out the piping design depends on your garden's watering needs.

Putting the pipe up on the rack can be done easily by one person. The best-suited piping materials are lightweight, and none requires strong physical strength to join them together. The best method is to secure each section (or row) of pipe to the frame as it is being installed, especially if you're using PB pipe. Rigid lengths of piping tend to stay in place during the installation process, but coiled piping moves around considerably. Duct tape or cable ties will keep your pipes in place.

Drilling Holes. Before drilling holes in the distribution pipes, which you can do before or after you install the pipe, you must decide how you want the garden watered. Do you want a low-pressure, slow drip over each row? Do you prefer a higher pressure that will spray water to both sides and the bottom? You must answer these types of questions before drilling the holes.

If you want water to drip out of the overhead piping slowly, drill a row of holes along the bottom of the pipe. Should you desire a long-distance spray of water, drill smaller holes on each side of the pipe. Remember, also, that the end of the water distribution piping, which is not connected to the water supply, will have to be capped off.

Water Source. Perhaps you want your irrigation system to have multiple watering functions. For example, you may want a slow drip over your onions and a fine spray blowing over your squash. Don't worry, you can have

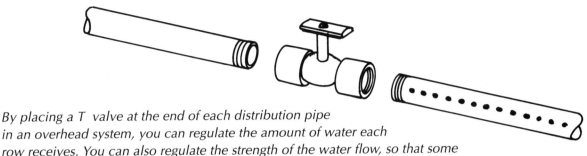

By placing a T valve at the end of each distribution pipe in an overhead system, you can regulate the amount of water each row receives. You can also regulate the strength of the water flow, so that some plants receive a slow drip while others receive a steady spray.

it. The installation process involves several tee fittings and valves.

Run one main distribution pipe along the pipe frame perpendicular to the direction of your garden rows. Install tee fittings in the main pipe, allowing branch distribution pipes to be installed over the rows. Place a valve near each tee outlet and extend the branch piping along your chosen path. Cap the open ends of all the pipes. Now you can turn each branch on and off at will, and you can drill different hole patterns in the piping to create a customized system. The cost and construction time of this system obviously will be more than a continuous pipe run, but your watering options are greatly enhanced.

Creating a Wooden Frame

Building a wooden frame uses a different construction method and, obviously, different materials than a pipe frame. Pressure-treated wood is the material of choice for a wooden frame. This green-looking wood will last much longer when exposed to the elements than untreated wood. It is not mandatory that treated wood be used, but if you want your frame to stand firm for years to come, treated lumber is a good investment.

Advantages of a Wooden Frame

~ Very sturdy

~ Can be bolted together for quick removal and reinstallation

~ Provides a nailing surface for cosmetic add-ons

Disadvantages of a Wooden Frame

~ May be expensive

~ May rot, unless pressure-treated lumber is used (which is not suitable for vegetable gardens)

~ Installer may suffer from splinters

~ Pressure-treated wood is heavy to work with

~ May attract wood-infesting insects, although this is not likely with pressure-treated lumber

SURFACE AND OVERHEAD IRRIGATION

Pressure-treated lumber is considerably heavier than small-diameter PVC pipe. While some people will be able to manage the lumber by themselves, other folks will want a helper. Wood also produces splinters, so a thick pair of work gloves is good insurance against puncture wounds.

Another difference in a wood frame is the type of saw used. While a carpenter's handsaw can be used for either lumber or PVC, cutting pressure-treated wood with a handsaw can get quite tiresome. Some type of electric saw, like a circular saw, makes the work less demanding physically, but power saws are much more dangerous to use. Caution must be observed at all times, especially if small hands are "helping" you (the kids or grandkids). **Unplug the saw after each use.** The last thing you want to see happen is one of those tiny fingers you love reaching for the trigger of a power saw.

Wearing eye protection is a good idea any time you are working in construction. When you are cutting and nailing wood, eye protection becomes more of a need than it would be when gluing pipe together. Sawdust can blow into your eyes. A nail that is hit poorly with a hammer can fly into space, and, perhaps, your face. **Safety procedures should not be taken lightly.**

In addition to the basic tools, a stable area to place the wood while it is being cut is necessary. Two 5-gallon buckets will get the job done. Standard sawhorses are fine, and folding tables made for construction projects are great. You can be creative, but make sure your support is strong and stable enough to prevent accidents while cutting.

When making a wood frame, the support posts should have dimensions of 4 inches by 4 inches, and will be installed at each corner of the irrigation boundary. The top rail of the frame can be made with 2-inch-by-4-inch lumber. The 2x4s either can be laid down flat or set up on their edge. If you plan to conceal your piping, stand the lumber on edge, to allow more space for concealment.

Construction Techniques

There are three basic ways in which to join your lumber: nails, although this method makes taking the frame apart difficult; screws, which are not necessary for structural integrity and disassembly can be a bother; and nuts and bolts, which are the most expensive option but allow you to take the frame apart and put it back together again easily. If I were building a frame for permanent installation, I'd use nails. For a portable frame, I'd use nuts and bolts, and lock washers will help to keep your joints tight.

Installation

Lay out the overall frame construction just as described in the instructions for a frame made from pipe (see pages 81–85). Of course, there will be no tee fittings used when working with wood. Support poles simply sit under the frame and butt into it. Use L brackets to attach vertical posts to horizontal wood members.

When the wood frame is complete, attach the piping using standard pipe clamps. These clamps fit over the pipe and are held in place with nails. When this is done, you may wish to conceal the piping.

Pressure-treated lattice comes in 4-feet-by-8-feet sheets and is expensive, but works very well as a finishing touch to a wood piping frame. The open weave of the lattice allows water to reach your plants and, at the same time, keeps the piping out of sight from a distance. The lattice is nailed or screwed directly to the underside of the wood frame. Additional wood supports probably will be needed at the outer frame for attaching the sheets of lattice. Keep this in mind while building your frame, because it is easier to install the inner supports before your piping is hung.

When it comes to having a practical irrigation system for your garden, overhead piping is hard to beat. By building your own frame and installing your own piping, the cost of the system is kept at a minimum. Since water from the system falls on the garden from above, it is much like rain. As practical as this system is for gardens, underground and surface systems work better for lawns. Appearance is much more important to a lawn-watering system. The area requiring watering also tends to be larger and have more uniform needs. These systems are addressed in the following chapter.

Installing Piping with an Overhead Wood Frame

1. Start at the water source and work to the end of the irrigation system.

2. Make connection at water source and extend piping over the framework.

3. Secure all piping as it is installed.

4. Use appropriate pipe fittings when making turns.

5. Install cut-off valves as desired.

6. Install a cap or plug on the terminal end of the piping.

7. Inspect piping for any kinks, twists, or tight turns.

8. Open the main water valve and fill the system with water.

9. Inspect system for leaks.

10. Put system into operation.

SURFACE AND OVERHEAD IRRIGATION

~ 8 ~

Buried Irrigation Systems for Lawns and Gardens

BURIED IRRIGATION SYSTEMS ARE ideal for lawns and good for some gardens. One big advantage to having a buried irrigation system in your lawn is its appearance — or lack of it. Since the system is installed below turf, it doesn't create an ugly fixture on your lawn. In fact, it's difficult to tell the system is there, unless it is in use.

Buried irrigation pipes in a garden are not as practical as they are in a yard, since gardens are often plowed and tilled over every year. A series of buried pipes can create an obstacle course. A buried system is fine for a flower garden, but may not be the best choice for irrigating a vegetable garden.

A buried sprinkler system is expensive, even if you install it yourself. There are many possibilities to consider when deciding on an in-ground sprinkler system.

If you already have shopped for an underground system, you know that the number of available choices is staggering. No wonder homeowners are often perplexed by lawn irrigation. This chapter is designed to clear up the confusion by giving an overview of the many types of in-ground systems.

Most of the irrigation systems discussed up to this point are easy to understand and don't call for extensive controls and wiring, or a vast knowledge of mechanical skills. High-tech, underground systems are different.

There are so many different installation possibilities for commercially offered sprinkler systems that it is not practical to describe each one in great detail. Instead, I will touch on the basic points of designing, installing, and using underground sprinklers. This information, however, may not apply to the particular type of system you have or plan to install. Much of the information is generic enough to be used with various types of systems, but in some cases, you may find discrepancies between these instructions and those of the manufacturer of your equipment. Follow the manufacturer's instructions.

The design and installation of an underground piping system for use with sprinklers can be quite complicated. For some people, even the pipe sizing is overwhelming, let alone the excavation of trenching to allow for installation, which poses its own set of problems. Unless you have experience, you might very well want to hire professionals to install this type of system. In this one book, I cannot give you complete information on how to build and install all of the various underground irrigation options available to you, or anticipate all the obstacles you may encounter. However, I can make you aware of the various components used in almost any underground sprinkler system and the role that each plays in the successful irrigation of your lawn or garden.

Design Considerations

When dealing with an expensive, underground sprinkler system, design considerations take on new importance. Much of this information applies to other types of irrigation systems as well, but it is most critical with an underground sprinkler system. This information is quite technical, but following is a general explanation.

Design Factors To Consider
When Laying Out An Irrigation System

~ Precipitation rate

~ Type of soil being irrigated

~ Absorption rate of soil being irrigated

~ Topography of irrigated area

~ Type of irrigation system to be used

~ Water-pressure requirements of any particular irrigation system

~ Available water sources

~ Time required to install system

~ Quantity of water available for irrigation

~ Method of installation (overhead, underground, mobile)

~ Equipment needed for installation (such as a rented trenching machine)

~ Cost of installation

~ Your own qualifications to perform the installation

WATERING SYSTEMS FOR LAWN AND GARDEN

Precipitation Rate

There are many basic concerns when designing any type of irrigation system, such as cost and availability of water. Another potential issue, depending upon topography and soil conditions, is runoff water. Finally, uniform irrigation and the control of diseases are of concern. For all of these possible problems, there is one root cause: the precipitation rate.

A precipitation rate measures the number of inches of rain falling on a given area in one hour. A high precipitation rate is one inch of water per hour, or more. An irrigation system is a substitute for rain. Therefore, you must deal with precipitation rates.

If the soil on your property does not accept water well, you must avoid a high precipitation rate. If you don't, there will be excessive runoff and possible erosion. On the other hand, if your land soaks up water like a sponge, you must provide a greater precipitation rate to keep your grass and plants watered properly, which, of course, means you must know a little about the ground that you are watering.

Let's assume that your lawn is level, so that runoff is not likely to be a problem. Further assume that the consistency of your soil is coarse. The rough texture of the soil will result in a fast absorption rate, meaning that you must produce a higher precipitation rate. Given these circumstances, what type of sprinkler system will work best?

When a **high precipitation rate** is needed, two sprinkler choices most often come to mind: fixed-spray sprinklers and bubblers. A third choice could be a microspray sprinkler. Other types are not as well suited to the needs of a high precipitation rate. By using one of these three sprinklers, you can operate the system for a shorter time than with another type of sprinkler while receiving good results. This is cost effective in that the system is not operating for extended periods of time.

Suppose that you need only a **moderate precipitation rate** for most of your irrigation season, but there are occasions when a higher rate is needed. A microspray sprinkler best serves these needs. A microspray head can operate in all three precipitation rates: low, medium, and high. A low rate is considered to be ½ inch of water per hour, and a medium rate runs between ½ and 1½ inch of water per hour.

If your watering needs will not exceed a medium precipitation rate, you have five basic choices available in sprinkler heads:

~ Rotating-Stream Heads
~ Stream-Spray Heads
~ Impact-Rotor Heads
~ Gear-Rotor Heads
~ Pop-Up Heads

Sprinkler Types

Sprinkler heads can be grouped into three rating categories: low precipitation, medium precipitation, and high precipitation.

Sprinkler heads with low precipitation rates are best suited for difficult topography, such as steep and hilly lawns. With a gradual dispersement of water, runoff will not be such a problem. This is also true if your soil does not perk well. Perking is the length of time it takes for soil to absorb water.

Medium precipitation rate sprinklers are often used under the same conditions as high precipitation rate sprinklers, but the medium-rate units are operated for longer periods and

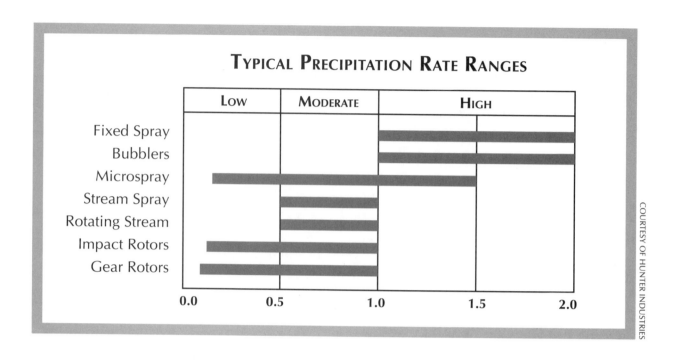

give an option of varying the water fall rate, eliminating the risk of erosion and runoff in borderline situations.

Sprinklers rated for high precipitation are used when runoff is not a problem. These heads can throw out a lot of water in a short time. As long as the irrigation area is relatively level and the soil accepts water generously, this type of head is ideal.

Two Factors for Precipitation Rates

When designing a sprinkler system, there are two factors to consider about precipitation rates. One is the **direct precipitation rate,** which refers to the dispersement capability of a single sprinkler, and the other is **system precipitation rate,** which refers to the performance of all sprinkler heads within a given system, in other words, how much water is being applied to the total area being irrigated. A sprinkler system doesn't use identical sprinkler heads in all locations. Installing different types of heads in different spots allows watering versatility.

In calculating a system precipitation rate, the result is most accurate when all system heads are producing similar rates of water. If extreme differences exist among the types of heads being used, the rate may be inaccurate, which can result in wet and dry spots.

Calculating the Running Time

Before you can design a system to maximum efficiency, you need to calculate the running time of the system, based on precipitation rates. If you are not familiar with precipitation rates, you cannot possibly gauge the running time needed for an irrigation system.

The United States Department of Agriculture and your county Cooperative Extension Service office can provide you with specific infiltration rates for various types of soil, such as in the chart next page. If you are unsure of

WATERING SYSTEMS FOR LAWN AND GARDEN

| SOIL TEXTURE | MAXIMUM PRECIPITATION RATES (INCHES PER HOUR): | | | | | | | |
| | 0 to 5% slope | | 5 to 8% slope | | 8 to 12% slope | | 12% + slope | |
	Cover	Bare	Cover	Bare	Cover	Bare	Cover	Bare
Coarse, sandy soils	2.00	2.00	2.00	1.50	1.50	1.00	1.00	0.50
Coarse, sandy soils over compact subsoils	1.75	1.50	1.25	1.00	1.00	0.75	0.75	0.40
Uniform light, sandy loams	1.75	1.00	1.25	0.80	1.00	0.60	0.75	0.40
Light, sandy loams over compact subsoils	1.25	0.75	1.00	0.50	0.75	0.40	0.50	0.30
Uniform silt loams	1.00	0.50	0.80	0.40	0.60	0.30	0.40	0.20
Silt loams over compact subsoil	0.60	0.30	0.50	0.25	0.40	0.15	0.30	0.10
Heavy clay or clay loam	0.20	0.15	0.15	0.10	0.12	0.08	0.10	0.06

The maximum precipitation-rate values listed are as suggested by the United States Department of Agriculture. The values are average and may vary with respect to actual soil conditions and condition of the ground cover.

COURTESY OF HUNTER INDUSTRIES

what type of soil you have, take a sample of it to your local Extension Service office or lab.

Determining Where Sprinklers Should Be Installed

The decision about where and how many sprinklers to install is best left to professionals. Even if you plan to install the system yourself, the cost of paying for competent design consultation up front can save you a lot of money in the long run. However, since I'm sure some people want to know how a system is laid out, I will share some of the formulas used by professionals.

Determining the Precipitation Rate

There are two considerations in developing a plan for spacing sprinkler heads: how far apart to set up rows of sprinklers, and how often in each row a head should be installed.

Some systems are laid out in a square-spacing pattern, and others incorporate a triangle-spacing pattern. The precipitation rate of a sprinkler system is inversely related to head and row spacing. Assuming that the sprinkler flow remains constant, *increasing* the head or row spacing *decreases* the precipitation rate, while *reducing* the head or row spacing *increases* the precipitation rate.

The following formulas may seem complicated. However, if you follow the instructions carefully, I think you will be able to do the math and compute your own sprinkler needs.

Single Sprinkler. To determine the precipitation rate for a single sprinkler, do the following calculations.

1. Multiply 96.25 times the gallons of water per minute for the sprinkler head. The 96.25 figure remains constant in this formula for converting gallons per minute (gpm) to inches

Improving Your Lawn's Water-Storing Ability

If you water your lawn two or three times a week just to keep it from turning brown, there are things you can do to turn a barely passable lawn into a lush one. The key is to improve your soil. By adding organic matter, you can improve your soil's water-storing ability.

Organic matter such as peat moss helps sandy soils to absorb more water and clay soils to drain better and move the moisture down to the grass roots. Organic matter comes in many forms: manure, straw, grass clippings — anything that adds bulk carbon to the soil. But peat moss is easy to work with, doesn't smell, and is easily available in hardware stores and supermarkets as well as lawn and garden centers.

Getting peat moss into your soil before you seed a new lawn is easy. Just spread it two inches deep on top of the soil and till it into the top six inches of soil. Getting peat moss into your soil when a lawn is already growing is a bit more difficult. Follow these steps for lawn renovation if your old lawn has a drinking problem and needs peat moss treatment.

1. Aerate the problem lawn by removing plugs of soil. You can either hire out the job to a professional or rent the right power tools to do it yourself. If you have an older lawn that needs thatching, now's the time to do it.

2. Rake up the thatch and soil plugs left lying on the grass after the above treatment.

3. Drag a bale of peat moss to the middle of the lawn. Cut it open and shovel out the contents, leaving little piles all over the lawn.

4. You may need to spray the lawn and peat moss with a fine mist of water to keep the piles from blowing away while you work.

5. Using the widest rake you can find, level the piles so that the entire lawn gets a half-inch top dressing of peat moss. Try to work the peat moss down into the holds left by the aerating machine.

6. If water tends to sit on top of your soil, add sand mixed half-and-half with the peat moss.

7. If your soil is sandy and water runs right through it, mix packaged, weed-free steer manure with the peat moss.

You can repeat this treatment every spring until you have worked a large amount of peat moss into the soil.

Excerpted from *Tips for Carefree Landscapes* by Marianne Binetti (Garden Way Publishing, 1990).

per hour. For the gpm rate, look on your sprinkler head. This formula is based on a sprinkler head that gives a full circle of coverage. For example, if your sprinkler has a listed rating of 6 gpm, then 96.25 x 6 = 577.5 inches per hour.

2. Multiply in feet the distance between the sprinkler heads in each row by the distance between the rows. For example, if there are 10 feet between each row of sprinkler heads, and the sprinkler heads are spaced 5 feet apart within each row, then 10' x 5' = 50'.

3. Divide the first number, 577.5, by the second number, 50, to get the precipitation rate per hour, 11.55 inches. In this example, obviously, the heads and rows are too close together. This much water would result in excessive runoff and possible erosion.

Since not all sprinklers are designed to give a full circle of coverage, there is another formula for figuring the precipitation rate in such cases.

1. Multiply the constant number 34,650 by the gpm rating for your sprinkler head. For example, if the gpm is 6, 34,650 x 6 = 207,900.

2. For the second step, you must know the arc of coverage provided by your sprinkler head. Multiply the arc times the head spacing times the row spacing. Assume the arc coverage is 180°, the space between sprinkler heads is 5 feet, and the space between rows is 10 feet. Then, 180 x 5 x 10 = 9000.

3. Divide the first number by the second number: 207,900 ÷ 9000 = 23.10. What would happen if we decided the arc of the sprinkler is a full 360 degrees? The first number would

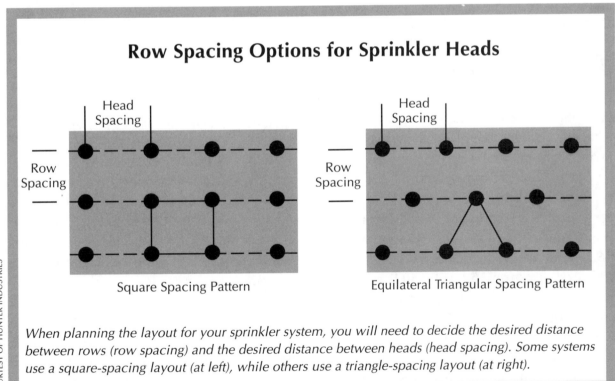

When planning the layout for your sprinkler system, you will need to decide the desired distance between rows (row spacing) and the desired distance between heads (head spacing). Some systems use a square-spacing layout (at left), while others use a triangle-spacing layout (at right).

BURIED IRRIGATION SYSTEMS FOR LAWNS AND GARDENS

be the same, 207,900. The second number would be 360 x 5 x 10 = 18,000, and 207,900 ÷ 18000 is 11.55, the same answer we arrived at in the example on page 95.

As another example, consider a full-circle sprinkler that delivers 5 gpm. With sprinkler heads spaced 20 feet apart, and rows 20 feet apart, what will the precipitation rate be? To find out, multiply the constant, 34,650, times the gpm rating, 5. The answer is 173,250. The arc (360 degrees) times the head spacing (20') times the row spacing (20') = 144,000; 173,250 ÷ 14,400, we come up with a precipitation rate of 1.20 inches per hour.

After figuring the rates for individual sprinklers, you can do a calculation for the entire area to be irrigated. This is necessary if you will be using sprinkler heads that do not maintain a consistent arc, flow rate, or spacing, which is not uncommon. Often different types and head style are used in a single system.

Sprinkler System. The precipitation rate for a complete system is determined by multiplying the constant number 96.25 by the total gpm of the system. Divide this number by the total number of square feet being irrigated to arrive at the precipitation rate.

For example, say that you have various types of sprinkler heads running at different gpm ratings. The total of all these gpm ratings added together is 46. The first step is: 96.25 x 46 = 4427.5. The surface area being irrigated measures 35 feet by 50 feet. To get the square footage, multiply the width by the depth: 35' x 50' = 1750'; 4427.5 ÷ 1750 = a precipitation rate of 2.53.

As you know, very few conditions will tolerate a precipitation rate in excess of 2 inches per hour, so the design should be altered to lower the precipitation rate. This can be done by using sprinklers with lower gpm ratings, or by eliminating some of the sprinklers. Keep in mind, however, that the precipitation rate does not reflect the uniformity with which water is delivered. To avoid dry or wet spots, you must keep the overall coverage from all sprinklers in mind.

Obtaining Balanced Coverage

When designing a sprinkler system, it is very important to ensure balanced water coverage. If the sprinkler heads are not matched and installed properly, the system will produce both wet and dry spots, neither of which is desirable. If a system is not balanced and dry spots occur, people often extend the running time of their sprinklers to compensate for the dry area. This results in applying too much water to most of the irrigation site in an attempt to save a small section from dying out.It is very important to consider even distribution of water when planning a system.

Matching Precipitation Rates

By matching the precipitation rates of all sprinklers used in a system, you can avoid hot spots. Matching precipitation rates means checking to see that all sprinklers in the system have the ability to cover an area with a flow rate equal to other sprinklers installed in the system. For example, a sprinkler that covers a 180-degree arc might be running at 2 gpm. If a full-circle sprinkler were to be used in conjunction with the half-circle sprinkler, the flow rate for the full-circle unit would have to be 4 gpm. This is a simple rule of thumb: If the arc of coverage doubles, so must the flow rate.

For example, assume you will be installing three types of sprinkler heads in your system. One type covers an arc of 90 degrees, one spans 180 degrees, and one gives full-circle coverage. To install this type of system properly, you would provide a flow rate of 1 gpm to the 90-degree heads. The 180-degree heads would need a flow rate of 2 gpm, and the full-circle heads would need 4 gpm. Installed this way, you would have a matched system in terms of precipitation rates.

What would happen if you operated the entire system described above at a uniform flow rate of 4 gpm? Well, let's see.

The 90-degree heads will be covering their arcs with a full 4 gpm. The 180-degree heads would produce a coverage with a rate of 2 gpm, half that of the 90-degree heads. Trouble is already starting. The area watered by the 90-degree heads is going to receive twice as much water as that watered by the half-circle heads. Add the full-circle heads, which are watering at a rate of 1 gpm, and you've got wet spots and dry spots.

There are only two good ways to avoid this problem. The first is to use a matched system, as we describe earlier. The second is to use controls and valves to adjust the running time on the various sprinklers. For example, run the half-circle sprinklers twice as long as the 90-degree sprinklers, and full-circle sprinklers one-quarter the amount of time allowed for the 90-degree heads. All in all, using a matched system is the best way to avoid this type of problem.

Matched Precipitation Rate System

● 4 GPM Full-circle head
◑ 2 GPM Half-circle head
○ 1 GPM Quarter-circle head
⊗ Irrigation Control Valve
– – Irrigation Main Line
(POC) Point of Connection

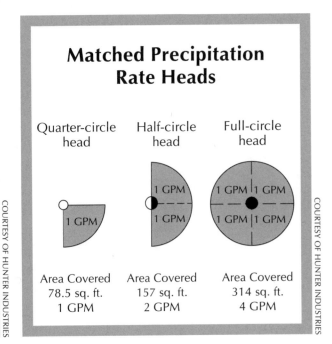

Matched Precipitation Rate Heads

Quarter-circle head — 1 GPM — Area Covered 78.5 sq. ft. 1 GPM

Half-circle head — 1 GPM / 1 GPM — Area Covered 157 sq. ft. 2 GPM

Full-circle head — 1 GPM | 1 GPM / 1 GPM | 1 GPM — Area Covered 314 sq. ft. 4 GPM

BURIED IRRIGATION SYSTEMS FOR LAWNS AND GARDENS

As I'm sure you've started to see, designing an irrigation system can be complicated. For a first-time designer, the task can be intimidating. This is why I recommend talking with local professionals in the design of your system.

Once you have determined the precipitation rates and arcs of coverage needed to adequately water your area, draw a layout plan on graph paper detailing the exact placement of various types of sprinkler heads, as shown.

Selecting Sprinkler Heads

A wide array of sprinkler heads is available, ranging from light-duty to industrial use. Since this book focuses on residential lawns and gardens, I will not bother with the commercial-grade heads, but will explore several types of sprinklers suited to residential needs.

In your search for the perfect sprinklers, you're going to have to thumb through a lot of brochures, just to see the many possibilities available. As I write, I have brochures from several manufacturers at my side and I know

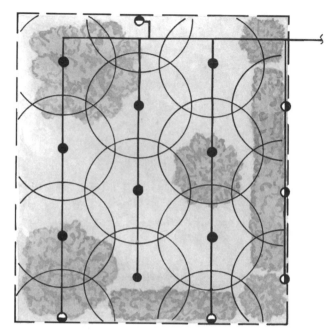

Make a layout plan for placement of sprinkler heads before you begin installing the system. This should show the exact location of various types of heads to meet the watering needs of your particular landscape.

sprinkler systems, but even so, it's hard to pick what's best from so many choices. Here's my summary of some of the features and benefits of various available models.

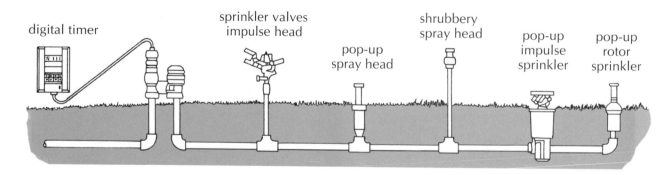

In designing an underground sprinkler system, you will find a wide selection of sprinkler head styles to choose from, depending on your budget and specific needs.

Gear-Driven Models

One of the more attractive gear-driven sprinkler heads for residential and light commercial use is available in three models: shrub, 4-inch pop-up, and 12-inch pop-up. The 12-inch pop-up can rise out of the ground a full foot and spray water over low-growing plants to reach taller plants and sloped areas. When the irrigation cycle is complete, the whole thing retracts back into the ground. This is an unusual feature, and one that can come in handy for many applications.

The 12-inch pop-up head can discharge as little as ½ gpm or as much as 14.4 gpm. It can work with a feed pressure range of 30 to 70 psi, well within the range of any household water supply. It connects to a ¾-inch male adapter, which keeps pipe costs down. There is a rubber cover that protects the sprinkler,

and the arc of spray is adjustable from 40 degrees up to 360 degrees. There is a filter to catch debris in the water before it harms the mechanisms of the sprinkler. Another feature is an optional drain check valve, which conserves water by keeping it in the system at the end of an irrigation cycle.

This pop-up head has a versatile nozzle selection, with 12 different, interchangeable nozzles. With this selection of nozzles, it is easier to maintain uniform coverage and avoid dry spots. If you don't want the selection of 12 standard nozzles, you can opt for a unit with 7 low-angle nozzles.

Another available gear-driven sprinkler head is available in four models: shrub, 4-inch pop-up, 6-inch pop-up, and 12-inch pop-up. This head attaches to ½-inch pipe and will run on pressure as low as 25 psi. The arc is adjustable from 40 to 360 degrees, and the

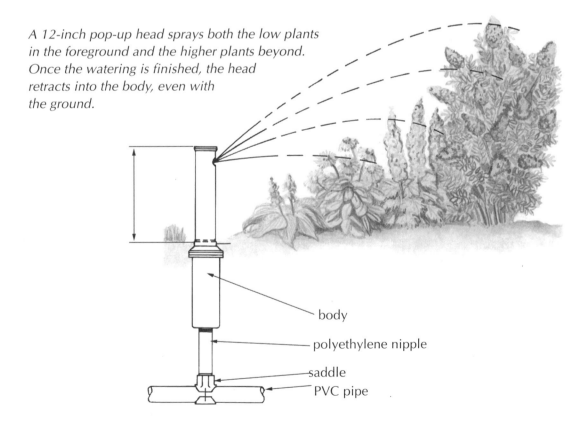

A 12-inch pop-up head sprays both the low plants in the foreground and the higher plants beyond. Once the watering is finished, the head retracts into the body, even with the ground.

body

polyethylene nipple

saddle

PVC pipe

BURIED IRRIGATION SYSTEMS FOR LAWNS AND GARDENS

nozzles are color coded for easy identification. A two-year warranty is standard issue on this type of head.

Models for Odd-Shaped Plots

Some lawns and gardens are odd shaped, which can make it difficult to get uniform water coverage from a sprinkler system. What is an odd-shaped lot? It may be one shaped like a triangle. This type of shape requires the use of various types of sprinkler heads to cover all of the turf efficiently. Another example of an odd-shaped lot could be one with a steep slope to it. The coverage angle of sprinkler heads varies, and this allows you to customize a design that will work with any type of topography.

There is a sprinkler head available that allows for arc control from 1 degree to 335 degrees. With this adjustment range, you can meet the water needs of any part of an odd-shaped plot. This particular sprinkler delivers anywhere from 0.2 to 5.3 gpm, connects to ½-inch pipe, and runs on water at pressure ratings from 20 to 40 psi.

Bubblers

A bubbler head can provide long, deep-soaking coverage in small areas. It is ideal for planters and tree wells when proper drainage is available. Some models offer a pressure-compensating device that allows a constant rate of flow from the bubbler even when the intake pressure varies. The operating range of delivery for these bubblers runs from 0.25 gpm to 1.5 gpm, and they run at intake pressures of 15 to 90 psi.

As you begin to shop for the sprinkler system, you'll quickly become aware of the great diversity of sprinkler heads available. There are so many possibilities that it is not feasible to cover them all in this book. I recommend checking out each manufacturer's line of products, comparing them to each other, and becoming accustomed to the phrases and terms being used.

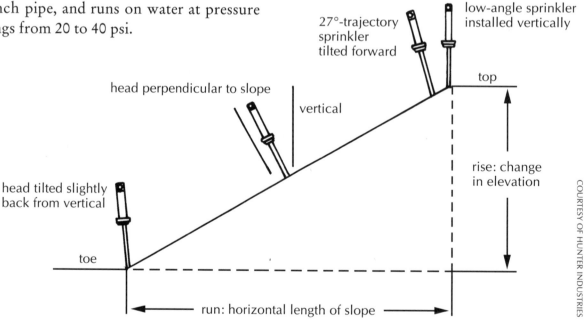

Sprinkler heads and angles can be customized to meet the watering needs of a sloped or odd-shaped lot. Here, the heads have been placed at angles to maximize the efficiency of each head.

Selecting Controls And Valves

Controls and valves are key elements in a buried irrigation system. If these devices fail, so will your irrigation equipment. Just as there is plenty to choose from in the way of heads, so is there a broad selection of controls and valves available. Again, this is an area where I recommend shopping around. The controls and valves are the heart and lungs of your system, so don't pinch pennies too tightly when making a buying decision.

Installing a Sprinkler System

The actual installation of a commercially purchased buried irrigation system may be beyond your capabilities. This is not to say that you can't do portions of the work, but parts of the job get quite technical. For example, you might feel perfectly comfortable with the plumbing phase of the job, but not able to handle the electrical side of the work. While it is possible for homeowners to install their own underground irrigation systems, it is often wiser to retain professional help, at least for certain parts of the work.

All in all, installing an underground irrigation system is not difficult. The hardest part is designing an effective system, and the wiring can be tricky. If you choose to hire a contractor to do the job for you, this chapter will help you to supervise the work in a more meaningful way. If you plan to do the job yourselves, you now have enough information to get well on your way. It will, however, probably be helpful for you to talk with local professionals and suppliers of sprinkler systems. These experts can assist you in designing your system and picking your equipment.

Selecting Pipe

Once you have a drawing of where you will place your sprinklers, you are ready to decide on what type of pipe to use. There are three common choices: PVC, polyethylene (PE), and polybutylene (PB). I have discussed the qualities of these pipes in Chapter 6. My favorite is polybutylene. However, there are some

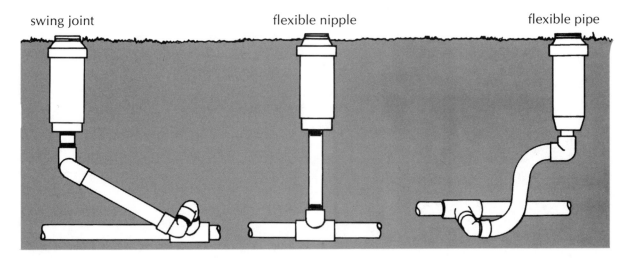

swing joint   flexible nipple   flexible pipe

Three types of sprinkler head installation

distinct advantages to each type of pipe when used in underground applications, as I'll review.

Durability When Frozen

Unless you bury your pipe below the frost line, you should drain all water from it before freezing temperatures hit. If the pipe is installed with a slight grade on it and you install drain valves, this can be done by gravity. PVC and CPVC pipes are rigid. If you want a system that can be drained by gravity when the watering season is over, rigid pipe is best. Flexible piping, such as PB and PE piping, will develop bellies and pockets of water that won't be able to drain naturally.

However, movement in the ground can cause even rigid pipe to move, creating level or low spots where water will not drain properly. To be safe, the best way to evacuate a piping system is by applying air pressure. With drain valves open and an air compressor connected to the system, it is possible to blow water out of the pipes. This is a much more dependable way of clearing the pipes of water.

While PVC pipe is easier to install on a grade than is flexible pipe, it is not as durable when frozen. If a section of PVC pipe is holding frozen water, it is likely that either the pipe will split or the fittings will swell and be pushed off the ends of the pipe. Since the reason for installing an irrigation system is to maintain a beautiful lawn, you certainly don't want to be digging it up every spring to fix leaks in the sprinkler piping.

PE and PB pipes are much more likely to survive freezing than is PVC pipe. Given equal circumstances, PE and PB pipes will expand without splitting when frozen. This is not to say that it is impossible for these pipes to split, but generally they won't. However, even if the pipe doesn't burst, constant freezing and thawing can weaken the pipe and the joints to a point where failure will occur. PB pipe installed with crimp rings and barbed fittings is the most resistant to damage from freezing. Depending on where you live, freeze-ups may not be of much concern. But, if you live in a cold climate, you should install drain valves and blow out the system with air each year, before frost sets in.

Working with PVC

I find PB pipe to be most user-friendly. PVC is certainly not difficult to cut or glue together, but it is temperamental. If the fitting or pipe being glued is the least bit dirty, the joint may be weak or contain a void. The joints also require considerable curing time. I have glued joints and left them for several minutes and still have been able to twist them and pull them apart. If it takes this long for the glue to set when undisturbed, consider what

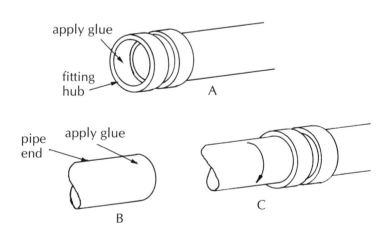

To join PVC pipe, apply glue to both the fitting hub (A) and the pipe end (B), insert pipe into fitting, and twist (C).

WATERING SYSTEMS FOR LAWN AND GARDEN

could happen as you install sections of piping along your trench. While working on the fittings for one sprinkler head, your actions may be weakening the joint on the last station you piped. Installing all of your piping only to find more water spraying out of your piping than your sprinkler heads is disheartening.

To join PVC pipe, make exact, square cuts. If the end of the pipe is cut on an angle, there will not be a full circle of pipe in the hub of the fitting, which weakens the joint. Next, always apply a cleaner/primer to both the end of the pipe and the fitting hub prior to gluing the joint. Be certain all areas to be glued are clean and dry. If the end of the pipe is wet, the glue will not set properly. Apply the glue liberally. Insert the pipe into the fitting and twist it. Rotating the pipe in the fitting evenly distributes the glue to all areas.

Some plumbers carry safety precautions one step further by wiping glue around the outside of the fitting after a joint has been made. This is somewhat effective, but it can also cause trouble because glue applied around the outside of the fitting does not create a strong seal. It may be enough to hold pressure during a test and even during some period of use, but if the primary seal in the joint is not good, the outer seal will blow out eventually. However, if you're going to have a leak, it is best to find it before you conceal the piping, so you don't have to use the wiping process.

PVC becomes very brittle in cold temperatures. Dropping the pipe on a hard surface, stepping on it, or hitting it with rocks as a ditch is backfilled can crack it. You probably won't be able to see the crack, but it will leak. Treat your PVC gently under all conditions, and be especially careful if you are working with it in cold temperatures.

Working with PE

PE pipe is joined with barbed insert fittings and hose clamps. The biggest challenge in working with PE pipe is to keep it from moving. The pipe comes in a coil, and it takes some effort to control it. I recommend unrolling the coil and stretching the pipe out to relieve any tension, being careful not to kink the pipe. You cannot make sharp turns and bends with it or it will kink quickly. If the pipe kinks, cut out the kink and install a coupling. Even though a kink can be worked out of the pipe, the wall of the pipe is weakened in that spot. Avoid taking chances on developing a leak by installing an inexpensive coupling and a few hose clamps.

Joints. PE pipe is easy to put together. Cut the pipe and remove any burrs around the end of it. Next, slide one or two hose clamps over the end of the pipe. One is all that is required, but I always double-clamp the joint to add a little extra insurance against future leaks.

barbed fitting

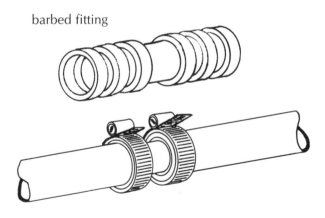

To join PE pipe, slide pipe ends over barbed fitting and attach hose clamp around each end.

BURIED IRRIGATION SYSTEMS FOR LAWNS AND GARDENS

Insert fitting. The next step is putting the insert fitting in place. In most cases, this is as simple as pushing the end of the fitting into the opening of the pipe. If the pipe is cold, you may run into two problems. First, the fitting may not go in easily, and, second, the clamps may not tighten up the way they should. These problems are easily solved by warming the end of the pipe with a handheld torch, heat gun, or hair dryer. Be careful not to overheat the pipe, and don't hold too much heat in one spot for too long or the pipe may melt or burn. As the pipe warms, it becomes softer and will accept the fitting more readily. Hose clamps will compress warm pipe much better than cold pipe. However, since you will probably be working on this project in warm weather, you shouldn't have to heat your pipe.

The cheapest fittings you can use with PE pipe are made of nylon, but I recommend using brass fittings. Either type will work well under average conditions. However, if the fittings become stressed, either from movements in the earth, such as frost heaves, or from rough handling during installation, nylon fittings may break. Also, you will be screwing sprinkler heads onto the threads of some of these insert fittings. One wrong turn on a nylon fitting can result in a crossthreaded fitting, requiring a replacement fitting. A metal insert fitting will not be nearly as susceptible to damaged threads.

Clamps. When you tighten the nose clamps, make sure they are positioned over the pipe in direct association with the ridges on the insert fitting. If you use double clamps, as I do, put one near the end of the pipe and the second one about ½ inch below the first one. Be careful as you tighten the clamps — I've seen many plumbers stab themselves with screwdrivers that slipped out of the groove.

I use a *torque wrench* to tighten hose clamps. It has a T handle and a little hub on the end that fits over the top of the screws, and works in a way similar to a rachet. This tool is faster and safer than a screwdriver for tightening hose clamps.

If you choose to work with my personal favorite, PB pipe, you are going to need a crimping tool. You can rent a crimping tool from a local tool rental store. You may also want to rent a special cutter that will make cleaner cuts and require less effort than a hacksaw.

Working with PB

PB pipe can be purchased in straight lengths or in long coils. I usually buy it in coils, but you may find the straight lengths a little easier to control. If you're working with a coil, unroll it and work any tension out until it lays flat on the ground.

Installing PB pipe is similar, in principal, to installing PE pipe.

1. Cut the pipe, slide one crimp ring over the end of the pipe (you only need one because they hold very well), and insert a copper barbed fitting.

2. Slide the crimp ring up the pipe until it is positioned over the ridges in the fitting.

3. Place the jaws of the crimping tool around the crimp ring, making sure the ring is centered in the jaws. If the crimp is made off-center, the joint will not be as sound.

4. Bring the handles of the crimping tool together until they stop and the crimp as been made. If you want to check to see that the crimping tool is working properly, you will need a go-no-go gauge, which is a simple little piece of metal that measures the crimp ring. If the ring is compressed properly, the gauge will fit over it. When a crimping tool is out of adjustment, the gauge will not fit over the crimped ring. The crimping tool rental agency should be able to provide you with a go-no-go gauge.

Installing Pipe

Digging trenches. Installing pipe requires trenches. These can be dug by hand or with a rented walk-behind trencher. I recommend the walk-behind trencher, especially if you need deep trenches that go below the frostline. Before you begin trenching, double-check your installation plan to make sure you will get the proper precipitation rate and coverage needed. You don't want to dig up your yard only to discover that the trenches are not spaced properly.

Laying pipe. Once the trenches are open, you are ready to lay the pipe. Remove any sharp objects, such as rough rocks, from the trench beds. For a first-class job, dig the trenches a little deeper than needed and add a layer of sand in the bottom to cushion the pipe. This is not necessary, but it is desirable in rough ground.

As you install the pipe, make sure it is supported by a solid base along its entire

Step 1: Dig the trenches.

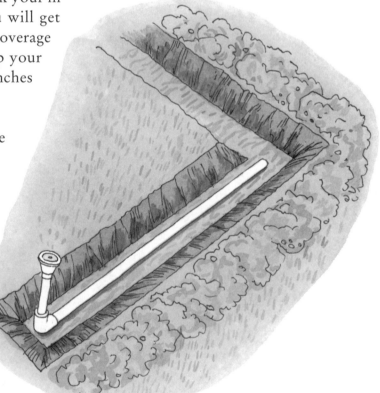

Step 2: Lay the pipes in the trenches.

length. This is especially important if you're using PVC or PE pipe. An unsupported section of PVC can snap during backfilling, and PE pipe can crimp badly. PB pipe is not as sensitive to this type of a problem, but it too should be supported fully.

Installing tee fittings. As you proceed with installation, you will be putting in tee fittings that will hold pipes and sprinkler heads, extending to a height determined by the type of sprinkler being installed. PE and PB pipe will not stand up straight by itself, but this is okay. Just let the risers lay over until the ditch is being backfilled, when you can support them with the fill. PVC will stand up on its own, but you must be careful not to hit it and break it off.

Step 3: Install the tee fittings.

Installing valves. Join the pipe as described on pages 102-104. You will need some type of valve, depending on the layout and the type of system. For example, you may wish to install automatic drain valves at each sprinkler head. An automatic drain valve should be installed at least twelve inches back from the riser for the sprinkler head. The valve will be installed with a tee fitting that is turned so that the tee outlet is horizontal. You should put a crushed stone base under and around the drain valve to help the drainage.

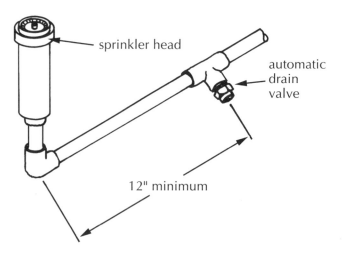

sprinkler head

automatic drain valve

12" minimum

Step 4: Install drain valves.

Other types of valves you might use include check valves, electric valves (which are connected to the system controller), manual drain valves, and so on. Exact determinations will depend on the system design and the manufacturer's recommendations.

After you have installed all of the pipe, test it for leaks. This can be done with water pressure or air pressure. All risers for sprinkler heads will terminate with threaded fittings, either male or female. You can screw caps or plugs, depending upon the types of threads available, on the riser stubs. This will seal the system and allow you to test it. The test should be done with a pressure that is at least equal to the maximum operating pressure. For instance, if your system will be working with a pressure of 40 psi, test at a minimum pressure of 40 psi. A higher test pressure will ensure that the system will stand up to its normal working pressure, but don't get carried away. Never test at a pressure exceeding 100 psi.

If a leak is detected, don't try to repair the joint. Cut it out and replace it. Once the pipe has been tested and found to be free of leaks, start the backfill process. Cover the pipe evenly and gently. Don't allow rocks or other sharp objects to rest against the piping. Routine vibrations in the pipe can cause it to rub against rough objects around it, resulting in holes in the pipe. Take special care in working around your sprinkler head risers. After you have backfilled to a point a few inches below the tops of your risers, it is time to install the sprinkler heads.

Installing Sprinkler Heads

The sprinkler heads used for residential purposes are usually equipped with inlet openings of either a ½-inch or ¾-inch diameter. These opening are normally provided with female threads. If you're installing ¾-inch pipe and connecting to ½-inch heads, you will have to install reducing fittings on the riser before installing the heads. The reducer simply converts the ¾-inch pipe to a ½-inch fitting. Depending upon your circumstances, short nipples (pieces of pipe threaded on both ends) may be needed between the reducer and the sprinkler head.

Whenever you are making a joint with threaded connections, you must use some type of thread sealant on the male threads. Apply it only to the male threads. It is generally recommended to use a tape-type thread sealant when installing sprinkler heads. Follow the suggestions provided by the manufacturer of your equipment. If you use tape, wrap it around the threads so that the tape gets tighter and the connection is made. Installing the tape backwards can result in it coming loose when the screw-connection is made. In other words, wrap the tape on the threads in a clockwise manner.

It is necessary to make screw-joints tight, but don't overtighten them, especially when working with nylon or plastic fittings. Excessive force can damage the materials. Besides, you can always give the joint an extra turn if it leaks, and that's a lot better than breaking a sprinkler head.

You will have to follow the recommendations of the product manufacturer in all aspects of your job. In general, most sprinkler heads are installed so that the housing/head is slightly above ground level, usually by about ¼ inch. Again, I must stress that you follow the manufacturer's recommendations in all aspects of your installation.

The Control Panel

The control panel for your system is its heart. It is also one aspect of the job that you might want to leave for professionals. If you are not familiar with wiring and controls, you shouldn't attempt to install it. I don't believe people who are not knowledgeable about electrical work should work with electricity. The risk is just too great.

I will not encourage or instruct you in how to work with electricity, nor can I tell you how your chosen control will be wired. However, I can give you an example of what you will be dealing with if you do your own wiring. Keep in mind, this is only an example and not all controllers are the same.

One of the controllers that I am most familiar with is a wall-mount model. It is fed, through conduit, with a 115-volt, 2-wire power feed, with a ground wire. The current is converted to 24-volt power before it leaves the controller, also through conduit.

As the wiring leaves the controller, there is one neutral wire. There is also a valve-control wire that powers the electric valve in the irrigation system. There are other optional wires available that can control pump circuits, other valves, and accessories. In basic terms, this is all there is to the wiring.

The principals of wiring a control panel are easy to understand, but the actual field work can be dangerous and confusing. If you are skilled enough to do your own wiring safely, you won't have any trouble interpreting the wiring diagram for your controller. If you can't read the wiring diagram, you don't know enough to do this part of the job safely.

A wall-mounted control panel provides a central place for programming the operation of your entire irrigation system.

WATERING SYSTEMS FOR LAWN AND GARDEN

Accessories

There are numerous accessories available for underground and automatic sprinkler systems. There are products designed to make installation easier, such as special wrenches, joints, riser service tools, and turf plug cutters, and there are devices that give you more control over the system, such as customized gauges. Components can also be added to your system that will enable it to sense rainfall and react accordingly. Once you have decided on a manufacturer, you can check their brochures to see exactly what accessories are available for the system you have chosen.

This is a typical wiring diagram for a sprinkler-system control panel. If you can't read the diagram, you should hire someone else to do this part of the installation.

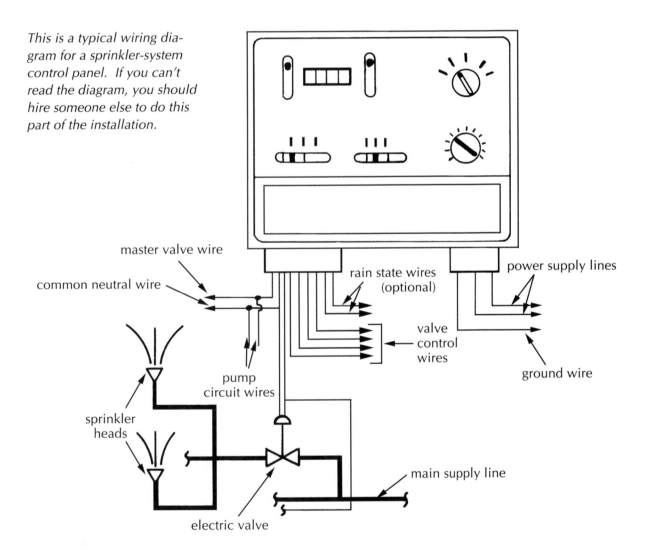

BURIED IRRIGATION SYSTEMS FOR LAWNS AND GARDENS

~ 9 ~

Having the Right Connections

THE RIGHT PIPING CONNECTIONS are an absolute necessity when installing an irrigation system. Even if code requirements in your area are lax on issues such as backflow protection, you cannot afford to cut corners when it may endanger your health. While you may not see any danger in connecting an irrigation system to your home's water supply, there is potential for disaster.

Aside from health issues, you must know how to install valves and fittings to get your irrigation piping connected to its water source. Do you know how to solder copper pipes and fittings? Would you know where to begin in making a connection between copper water pipes and polybutylene irrigation pipes?

If your system requires a pressure-reducing valve, will you know what type to buy and how to install it? There are many questions that can arise when you get to the stage of making final connections with your irrigation piping.

Since there are many irrigation systems available, there are a multitude of ways to connect them to a water supply. The methods used with a cistern are likely to be different from those employed with a municipal water supply. Tying into a pressure tank with a pump system is yet another possibility. All of these jobs can involve different types of pipe and different connection methods. This chapter offers an overview of common types of connections.

Backflow Problems

Backflow protection has gained importance over the past several years. When I entered the plumbing trade, backflow preventers were never used in residential plumbing. As people have become more educated in health risks, the requirements for backflow prevention have grown. Today, nearly every house plumbed to code has some type of backflow prevention.

What is backflow prevention? It is just as its name implies, a form of protection that prevents water from flowing backwards in a potable water system. It's important because it prohibits potable water pipes from becoming contaminated with chemicals or other materials which could be detrimental to human health.

Is backflow prevention really needed? Yes. While the need for such protection is rarely seen, the protection is priceless when it is called upon to do its job. Let me give you a couple of examples of how you can suffer from not installing backflow preventers on your piping.

Backflow from a Garden Hose

Consider the example of a simple garden hose you have connected to the outside faucet of your home. The hose bibb (faucet) is not equipped with a backflow preventer. After watering your garden plants, you decide to spray your potato plants to rid them of beetles. To do this, you install a pesticide bottle/sprayer on the end of your water hose. Just as you begin spraying the poison, you are called into the house because the water heater is leaking onto the basement floor. You set the sprayer down on the ground and rush into the house.

In the basement, you find a large puddle of water forming on the floor. You immediately go to the main water cut-off for your home and close the valve. Upon further inspection, you find that the water heater is beyond repair and must be replaced. Knowing what plumbers charge, you decide to save yourself a little money by draining the water heater while you are waiting for a plumber to arrive. However, as you drain the water heater, you are, unknowingly, contaminating the pipes which convey your drinking water.

Do you know what's going on? If you guessed that the poison in the bottle that is connected to the garden hose is being sucked back into the water pipes, you're right. When the water heater is drained, it creates suction in the potable water pipes. Since the garden hose is still connected to an open hose bibb, the contents of the hose are also drained. This creates a siphonic action pulling the pesticide into the pipes. Once the poison comes into contact with the potable water piping, the walls of the piping become contaminated. This disaster can be avoided by installing an inexpensive backflow preventer on the threads of a hose bibb.

A Faulty Check Valve

As another example, consider the case of an extensive garden irrigation system deriving water from the house well potable water supply. The irrigation system was designed so that you could mix plant food with the irrigation water, and that is what you are doing on this fateful day.

The irrigation system is running, producing a mixture of water and plant food for your vegetables when there is a power failure and your well pump cuts off. To make matters worse, the check valve on the system sticks in the open position. As a result, all of the plant food is sucked back into the household piping. With the check valve malfunctioning, water rushes back into the well, pulling a vacuum on the piping system. This causes the plant food to be sucked into the potable water system, contaminating the pipes.

Backflow Protection

When you install an irrigation system, install backflow preventers. These devices, for the purposes we are discussing, are not very expensive, and they can be one of the best investments you will ever make. There are a number of ways that a backflow problem can be caused. I've given you two examples of how easily pipes could become contaminated, and there are many other ways for it to happen. The installation of check valves and backflow preventers can protect you, but they can only do it if they are installed.

Hose Bibbs

All hose bibbs should be equipped with backflow preventers. Some types of hose bibbs are manufactured with a backflow preventer built right into them, others require installing one on their threads. A typical hose-bibb backflow preventer that screws onto the threads of the outside faucet costs less than $10. It has threads on the other end for connecting a garden hose. This is a very simple, inexpensive item, but it could save your life, or at least a lot of money.

In-Line Protection

In-line protection with a backflow preventer should be used on all pipes connecting your irrigation system to your potable water supply. This type of device costs less than $50, but is well worth it. An in-line backflow preventer is installed in a section of

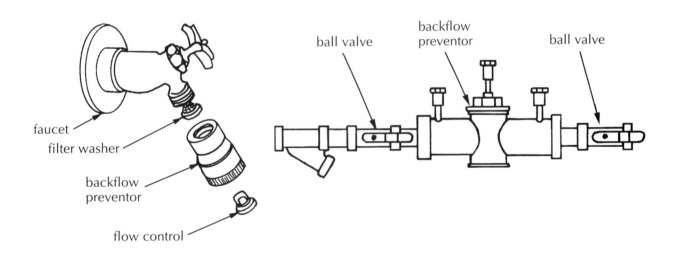

Backflow (or anti-syphon) prevention is important to have either on a hose bibb (at left) or as part of your in-line piping (at right). A backflow preventor keeps water from your irrigation system from flowing backwards into your potable water supply.

HAVING THE RIGHT CONNECTIONS

piping with the same principals used to install a coupling, union, or other fitting. If you have the skills needed to install your own piping, you have the ability to install this type of backflow preventer.

Added Insurance

A check valve can be installed in your piping as added insurance. This is a device that allows water to run through it in only one direction. For example, water could leave your home, pass through the check valve, and feed your irrigation system, but water from the irrigation piping could not run back past the check valve. While a combination of a check valve and an in-line backflow preventer is not necessary, it is wise. The check valve should be installed first, and the backflow preventer installed next. Check valves are available in different configurations and prices, with most of them costing between $10 and $20.

When installing an in-line backflow preventer or check valve, you must look carefully on the device for the word "inlet" or an arrow. The end of the device labeled "inlet" is installed on the piping going from your house to the irrigation piping. In other words, the inlet end is installed so that it is the end receiving the first water pressure.

Check valves and backflow preventers marked with an arrow should be installed so that the arrow indicates the direction of flow. In other words, the arrow should be pointing in the direction of your irrigation piping. If you don't observe this rule, your device will not function properly. For example, a check valve installed backwards will not allow any water to be delivered to the irrigation piping. If this happens, you have to remove the check valve and reinstall it with the arrow pointing in the right direction.

Pressure-Reducing Valves

Some irrigation systems require a reduction in water pressure. I discussed the operating pressure ranges for different types of irrigation equipment in Chapter 5. Most equipment will work effectively with normal household pressure, but for some equipment you may have to lower the water pressure by installing a pressure-reducing valve.

A pressure-reducing valve is installed in the pipe that supplies water to an irrigation system. Most of these valves allow a considerable range of adjustment. It is common to see the adjustment range running from 25 psi to 75 psi. If your irrigation equipment requires an operating pressure lower than your household pressure, a pressure-reducing valve is the answer.

Installation

Installing a pressure-reducing valve is no more difficult than working with any type of fitting. Some valves are provided with female threads and others are set up with connections

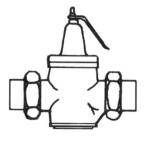

A pressure-reducing valve is necessary if your irrigation equipment requires a water pressure that is lower than your household water supply pressure.

meant to be soldered to copper tubing. If you are not working with copper piping, make sure to buy one with female threads.

Just as check valves are normally marked with a direction arrow, so are pressure-reducing valves. It is important to install the valve with the arrow pointing in the direction of your irrigation piping. The weight of some pressure-reducing valves is enough to require more support than standard piping. When you install such a valve, make sure that its weight is supported with a hanger or some other acceptable support, so that its weight doesn't create stress on the piping.

Water pressure regulators are also desirable with some types of irrigation equipment. These devices look similar to pressure-reducing valves, and they install in about the same way. Some have a range of adjustment equal to that of pressure-reducing valves, and others have a smaller range of adjustment. If the manufacturer of your irrigation equipment specifies a need for a regulator, follow the manufacturer's recommendations for a pressure setting.

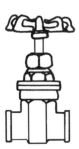

A cut-off valve should be installed where the irrigation piping meets the household piping so that the irrigation system can be shut off without affecting the water pressure in the home.

Cut-Off Valves

Cut-off valves should be installed at all points where irrigation piping meets household piping. These allow the water to the irrigation system to be cut off without affecting the water pressure in the home. While any type of cut-off valve will work, a gate valve or ball valve is preferable. These are full-flow valves that don't depend on washers to ensure a positive closing action, giving you better water flow and a more dependable cut-off valve.

Cut-off valves are made with different types of connections in mind. There are valves built with sockets to accept copper tubing for soldered joints. Some valves are made with female threads on either end. If you will not be using copper tubing, the valves with threaded connection ports are the ones to buy.

Connections for Frost Protection

Many irrigation systems are portable enough to be taken down after each growing season, eliminating a need for frost protection. Other systems, however, are complex and difficult to remove and must be protected against freezing weather.

If you are installing an underground irrigation system, you can minimize the risk of frozen pipes by burying the system below the frost line. This, coupled with the use of drain valves, normally provides adequate protection. However, there are times when it is not feasible to bury the piping at a sufficient depth to avoid freezing. This is often the case in Maine, where big rocks and bedrock are commonly encountered at shallow depths and where the frost line is about four feet deep. If

~ **115** ~

you are faced with this type of a situation, you must provide connections for clearing the system of all standing water when the irrigation season is over. The same is true for overhead irrigation layouts that are too much trouble to disassemble each year.

The best way to ensure that a system is free of standing water is to blow the water out of the pipes with air pressure. This is not a complicated procedure, as long as you planned for the need in advance and installed the proper connections. What are the proper connections? Well, first of all, you need drain valves that can be opened to release water from the irrigation piping.

Installing Drain Valves

For an overhead system, a drain valve is easy to access. You simply install a boiler drain wherever you want to drain the system, and when that time comes, open the valve by hand. Underground systems are not so easy to deal with. When you install drain valves in an underground system, you must make provisions for accessing the valves, which is usually done with a plastic box that sits over the valve and extends to ground level. By removing the cover of the box, you have direct access to the valve. You may need a special tool to operate the valve, but the box gives you the required access.

Valve boxes are molded in a way that allows them to sit over a section of pipe. Once the box is in place, the hole around the box is filled with dirt. These boxes are available in various heights to accommodate different frost lines. If the pipe is buried at a depth beyond reach, a valve is installed that can be turned on and off with a water key.

Air Valves

In addition to drain valves, your system must be equipped with a connection point for an air hose. There are several ways to do this. You can rig up a hose adapter that allows you to screw the hose from an air compressor onto the threads of a boiler drain. These are the same type of threads found on outside faucets. If you prefer to use a standard air chuck, you will have to create a connection that will accept an air valve. This is not a big job.

Let's assume that your irrigation piping has a ¾-inch diameter. You need to work your way to a point where an air valve with ¼-threads can be screwed into the system. To do this, you will use a series of reducing fittings. Your first reduction might go from a ¾-inch fitting to a ½-inch fitting. From there you could go down to a ¼-inch fitting. This will give you female threads of a size that will allow the installation of an air valve.

Air valves should be installed at the furthest point of the irrigation system. It is a good idea to install more than one. Another wise move is to install a standard cut-off valve between the irrigation piping and the air valve. This cut-off valve can remain in a closed position until you are ready to evacuate the system. Without such a valve, it is possible that water will leak past the air valve. For a few extra dollars you can have a solid valve that will not allow this to happen.

Working with Copper Pipe

I have described how to install various types of pipes in Chapters 5 and 6, but I haven't addressed working with copper pipe. While it is unlikely that you will use copper in making your irrigation system, it is very likely that your irrigation piping will tie into copper pipe for the water source, especially if that source comes from household pipes.

Some houses are plumbed with CPVC water pipes, and many newer homes have polybutylene pipe, but a majority of houses have copper water pipes. In connecting non-copper irrigation piping to copper water pipes you must have the proper adaptations for a connection and learn to solder or use compression fittings for making the actual connection.

Adapters

Assume that you have used polybutylene piping for your irrigation system and you are ready to connect the PB pipe to the copper pipe. To do this, you will need to cut out a section of the irrigation pipe to install a tee fitting. Shut off the water to the main water pipe before cutting. Once you have the main water supply shut off, open the faucets in your sinks, lavatories, and bathing units. If you have a valve in a position lower than where you will be making the cut, open that too, so that you drain as much water from the system as possible before cutting into the main water pipe.

There are two types of tee fittings: a standard copper tee, which works best, or a compression tee, if you can find one large enough to fit over the pipe you are using. If you are connecting to ½-inch (inside diameter) copper, a compression tee shouldn't be hard to find. Anything larger could prove troublesome to locate.

There is a difference in measuring systems that may be confusing if you're not aware of it. Soldered fittings and plumbing pipe are sized by the inside diameters, while compression fittings are sized by the outside diameter. For example, a pipe that uses ½-inch solder-type fittings will use ⅝-inch compression fittings; pipe that uses ¾-inch solder-type fittings will require ⅞-inch compression fittings. Just remember, compression fittings are sized for outside diameters and solder fittings are sized for inside dimensions.

Compression fittings connect to existing copper water pipes without soldering the joints, but they are more prone to leakage than are soldered joints. For this reason, I prefer soldered joints. If you are using a compression fitting with PB pipe, you shouldn't use a brass compression ferrule, because, when the compression nut is tightened too much, the sharp edges of a metal ferrule can cut into the walls of PB pipe. Use a nylon ferrule if you mate PB pipe to a compression fitting.

With a compression tee no other adapter is needed. With a standard solder-type fitting, you will need a conversion adapter. If barbed fittings and crimp rings are used to install PB pipe, the adapter used will be soldered into the tee outlet. The other end of the fitting will be a barbed insert. Once all soldering is done and the pipe and fittings have cooled, the PB pipe can be connected to the barbed adapter.

Compression fittings should not be used with PE pipe. The proper adaptation requires a standard tee fitting to be installed in the copper water main. A short piece of copper is placed in the tee outlet and a male or female adapter is soldered onto the end of this pipe. The result is a threaded connection point where an insert fitting can be attached. The insert fitting will screw into, or onto, the threaded fitting, allowing the PE pipe to be

HAVING THE RIGHT CONNECTIONS

connected to the insert end of the fitting. This same approach can be used when connecting CPVC pipe to copper.

Installing a standard solder-type tee is not a big job, but it can be frustrating, even for professional plumbers. If the pipe being connected is not empty of all water, soldering joints that won't leak is difficult. There are ways, however, to work around water and the steam created from it. To expand on this, let's go through the methods used to install a tee fitting, step by step.

Soldering Joints

Connecting irrigation piping to copper household piping with the best joints available requires making watertight solder joints. Soldering joints with copper pipe and fittings is a job that most anyone can learn to do with the following instructions.

1. Cut off all water to the pipe on which you will be working, and drain all fixtures and pipes as best as you can.

2. To prepare for making cuts for the tee fitting, hold the tee fitting up against the section of pipe you will be cutting. Notice that the tee has hubs on each end that flare out to be a little larger in diameter than the tee itself. The pipe should be cut so that it will extend fully into the hubs on each end of the fitting. Mark the cut locations on the pipe with a pencil. As a rule of thumb, ½-inch fittings will fit into the fitting for ½ of an inch, and ¾-inch fittings accept a ¾-inch length of pipe. If you are uneasy about making a perfect cut, you can cut more pipe than you need and use a coupling with the tee to put everything back together again.

3. Cut out a section of pipe for the tee to be installed. Copper pipe can be cut with a hacksaw, but the job is easier when you have a true copper cutter. These cutters have rollers and a cutting wheel. Inexpensive versions are sold in hardware stores, and even cheap copper cutters work better than a hacksaw. Cut the pipe as marked. Don't be surprised if a little water sprays out as you cut; this is normal. Once both cuts are made and the pipe section is removed, hold the tee in place to check for fit. If you find you removed too much, cut out another several inches of the pipe to make room for both the tee and a coupling.

In some cases, there is not enough play in a pipe for installing a fitting, such as when the

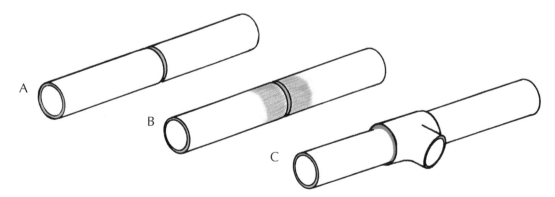

Connecting irrigation piping to copper household piping requires making a clean cut with a hacksaw (A), sanding the ends of the pipe with fine-grit sandpaper (B), and joining the pipe ends in a fitting (C).

pipe ends can't be moved back and forth enough to allow the fitting to be installed and the pipe to be seated in the hubs. If this happens, buy slip couplings (couplings without stops), so they can be slid along a length of pipe indefinitely. See Step 7 for further explanation.

4. Prepare your joint by sanding the ends of the pipe with a fine-grit sandpaper until the ends of the pipes are shiny from the end to a point beyond where the fitting hub will terminate. When the fitting is placed on the end of the pipe fully, there still should be some shiny pipe visible.

5. Clean the fitting with a special wire brush. If you don't have a brush, you can roll sandpaper around a pencil. Scrub the inside of the fitting until it shines.

6. After all joint areas are clean, apply a generous coating of flux to the fitting hubs and pipe ends with a small brush. Flux helps to clean the joint area and makes solder run around the joint. There are numerous brands on the market. Don't allow flux to get in your eyes, mouth, or cuts because it burns terribly.

With all areas coated in flux, put the pipe and fitting together. Make sure the pipe sinks all the way into the fitting hubs.

7. If you can't get the fitting onto the pipe ends, cut out several additional inches of pipe. Shine the end and apply flux. Slide a slip coupling over the pipe and slide it back until the end of the pipe is visible. At this point you have your tee installed on one pipe end and the slip coupling placed over the other pipe end. Measure between the tee and the exposed pipe end. Cut a piece of pipe that will sit in the tee and extend to within about ½ inch of the exposed pipe end. Clean each end of the pipe and coat them with flux. In-

stall one end in the tee. Now you have a short gap between the two remaining pipe ends. Slide the slip coupling down to bridge the gap.

8. This actual soldering of the joint is a little more difficult than the previous steps. You will need a torch and a roll of solder. The torch can be a hand-held propane type sold in hardware stores. The solder must be plumbing solder, not electronic solder, and should be lead-free.

Assuming there is no residual water in the pipe being soldered, begin by heating the tee fitting at one of its hubs. Hold the flame under the fitting at the point where the hub meets the tee. This is assuming you are soldering a horizontal pipe. If the pipe is vertical, hold the flame on either side of the fitting with the flame near where the fitting meets its hub. As you heat the fitting, you will see the flux begin to melt and the copper change color.

Assuming you are working with horizontal piping and that the flame is beneath the fitting, place the tip of the solder on the top of the tee, at the point where the pipe enters the fitting. If it doesn't melt and run

Soldering Vertical Joints

Vertical joints are no more difficult than any other type to solder. The heat and the flux will pull the solder up into the vertical hub. The key is to keep the heat near the point where the hub becomes the fitting. By doing this, the heat will pull the solder up or down, depending on which end of the fitting you are working with.

HAVING THE RIGHT CONNECTIONS

around the fitting immediately, remove the solder. Continue heating the fitting through this entire process. After heating the fitting a little longer, touch the solder to the pipe and fitting to see if it will melt. When the temperature is right, the solder will melt and run around the fitting.

If the pipe turns black, it is too hot and will not take a good solder joint. The key to successful soldering is in the temperature and preparation work. The prep work is easy enough, but you will have to experiment a little to learn when the temperature is right. If solder doesn't run smoothly around a fitting, dab on some more flux, around where the pipe and fitting meet. This will often solve the problem.

9. If your solder clumps and falls off the joint, or you see steam blowing out around a fitting, there is probably water in the pipe. If you have water in a pipe, you will have to take some steps to eliminate the problem. One way is to install a bleed coupling that has a vent hole in it. By removing the cap and rubber gasket from the vent hole, water and steam can escape, leaving you free to solder. If a bleed coupling isn't available, you can use a piece of bread to solve your problem, believe it or not!

Packing the soft center of white bread (no crusts!) into a pipe with your finger can stop the flow of trickling water long enough to allow a successful solder joint. Don't pack it too tightly, however. (As a rookie plumber, I once packed bread into a water line so tightly with a pencil that I obstructed the pipe and no water could flow into the fixture being served by the pipe!) After the joint has cooled, cut the water back on and flush the bread out of the system. Ideally, you should bleed the bread

out through a tub spout or outside faucet. Water will also dissolve the bread and allow it to pass through a sink faucet, but be sure to remove the aerator so the bread won't clog up the screen.

Pointers on Soldering

~ Always wear eye protection because hot solder can splash, bounce, and drip into your face.

~ Keep a fire extinguisher handy, since you never know when your torch may ignite some unexpected fire. If you are soldering close to a combustible material, like wood, put aluminum foil or some metal substance between the flame and the combustible material. To be on the safe side, you can even saturate the combustible material with water before you begin to solder.

~ Don't touch pipes, valves, and fittings that have been soldered recently since they retain the heat for several minutes and can inflict nasty burns.

~ Allow a few minutes after soldering is completed before turning on the water. If you turn the water back on and discover a leak, don't try to resolder the fitting. Cut it out and replace it.

Screw Joints

Screw joints are simple enough: You screw male threads into female threads. However, there are some rules to be followed. First of all, some type of thread sealant should be applied to the male threads before they are mated with female threads. A lot of plumbers prefer to use a tape sealant, which many manufacturers also recommend for their sprinkler heads and accessories. I prefer a paste-type thread sealant for most purposes, but when a manufacturer specifics tape sealant, use it.

When applying pipe sealant of any kind, only apply it to male threads, never to female threads. The way tape sealant is wrapped around threads can have a bearing on how well it works. Wrap the tape so that it becomes tighter as the joint is made. Putting the tape on backwards may cause it to come loose as the joint is made.

How Tight Is Tight Enough?

Screw joints should be tightened to a point where they don't leak, obviously. If you are working with nylon or plastic threads, tightening them too much can result in a broken set of threads. Make the fittings snug, but don't apply excessive pressure. Learning how tight is tight enough comes with experience. Use your own judgement, but be aware that one extra turn can result in a broken fitting.

Start all threaded fittings by hand and screw them in as far as you can without using a wrench to avoid crossthreading. Crossthreading can be a real problem when working with nonmetallic threads such as nylon and plastic. If the fitting is crooked when the tightening begins, the result will be ruined threads. So screw by hand as much as possible to keep the threads aligned.

Glue Joints with CPVC Pipes

If you have CPVC pipe in your house, your pipe connections will be glue joints. I discussed making glue joints earlier in reference to new installations using dry pipes. Cutting into existing CPVC pipes follows the same procedures, but you must be sure that water doesn't mess up the joints. If water runs too soon through a recently glued pipe, the result will be globs of glue and leaks.

After cutting the pipe, give it time to drain completely. Dry it out with a rag, if possible. Wait to watch for dripping and don't try to glue a joint until you are sure the water has drained completely. Other than that, the process will be the same as the procedures described on pages 102–105. One other word of caution: If you are installing screw fittings in CPVC, be careful not to break the pipe. I can't stress enough how easy it is to crack, snap, and break CPVC and PVC pipe.

Getting the Pipe into Your Home

Getting the irrigation feed pipe into your home requires special attention. If you're running a seasonal water line, it can enter the home aboveground. Underground piping, due to its depth, must come through a hole in the foundation of your home below ground level.

HAVING THE RIGHT CONNECTIONS

Making a Hole in the Foundation

Getting through the foundation depends on the type of material you are penetrating. Cinderblock is easy to get through with a cold chisel and a hammer. A rotary hammer drill also works quickly on cinderblock and brick. If, however, you have to go through an 8-inch concrete wall, a cold chisel won't work, and you'll be much better off renting an electric jackhammer. These tools can be rented at most tool rental centers, run on standard household current, and are light enough to hold up against the wall without undue stress. You may, however, wish to support the jackhammer with a stepladder to take some of the pressure off your arms.

Once you have a hole in your foundation, you need to install a sleeve. This is a pipe at least twice as large as the feed pipe providing your irrigation system with water. If you are running a ¾-inch feed pipe, your sleeve should be at least a 1½-inch pipe. If you don't sleeve your pipe, the foundation material may have a corrosive reaction on the feed pipe. It is also possible that the rough edges of a foundation will rub a hole in the feed pipe. Plumbing codes require sleeves, and they are good protection for your feed pipe.

Aboveground Entry to House

If your irrigation feed pipe is coming into your home aboveground, you can avoid penetrating the foundation. Drill through the siding and band board of your house with a wood-cutting bit, assuming you have wood or vinyl siding. If you have aluminum siding, a metal-cutting hole saw will be needed. This will get you through the siding and to the wood, where you can switch to a wood-boring bit. A sleeve is not necessary in this type of installation.

There is an alternative to boring a hole in the side of your house for an aboveground pipe. You can run the pipe to an outside faucet and connect to its threads. Adapters can be purchased to allow your feed pipe to screw onto the threads of the hose bibb. If you don't already have a backflow preventer on your outside faucet, put one on it.

Pitless Adapters

Pitless adapters are made for installing well pipes in drilled wells. This is not, however, the only practical use for them. They also work very well when used with aboveground cisterns.

Pitless adapters are made to mount in halves. One half on the inside of a well casing, or cistern, and the other half on the outside. To install, drill a hole in the well casing or cistern. The adapter seals the hole and provides threaded connection ports on both sides of the well casing or cistern. There is no better way to make a solid, watertight seal in this type of situation.

Pump Systems

Pump systems can be used to feed irrigation systems. If you are tying into an existing well system, you can use the same procedures discussed on page 45. When an independent system is used for irrigation, your connection method will be a little different, though not more difficult.

Assuming that a pressure tank is used with your pumping system (and one should be), there will be a threaded connection from your feed pipe to the irrigation pipe. The connection will be made by screwing a male or female adapter into, or onto, the waiting threads.

Potential Pitfalls

There are some pitfalls of which you should be aware. I've been working with pipe and fittings for over 20 years, and I've seen and made a lot of mistakes. While I can't protect you from all of the problems you may run into, I can certainly help you steer clear of some of the ones I've encountered.

Choosing the Wrong Feed Pipe

You can get yourself into hot water — literally — if you tie into the wrong water pipe. It's not too difficult to mistake a hot-water pipe for a cold-water pipe. They look the same, they're the same size, and, unless you feel the difference, the only way to know which is which is to trace the piping. Since I'm quite sure you don't want to spray your lawn or garden with expensive hot water, choose your feed pipe carefully. The safest way to be sure that you are dealing with a cold-water pipe is to trace the pipe back to its source. This is the only way to be sure that you are tying into the pipe you want. If you don't think you could make this mistake, let me tell you about a professional plumber I knew who made an even bigger mistake.

Most houses in Maine are heated with hot-water baseboard heat. Water is heated in a boiler and delivered to the heating units through copper tubing, the same type that is frequently used for potable water pipes. On this particular occasion, the plumber was

Putting All the Pieces Together

Putting all of the pieces together to get your irrigation system operational can take some time. Depending on your system, the job could take as little as an hour or as long as a weekend. Don't rush, and don't cut into your main water pipe when supply stores are closed or time is short. If you run into unexpected trouble, your whole house could be without water for a while.

Assuming that you are going to start your job on a Saturday morning, the steps might be as follows.

1. Gather all the materials you will need. Have a gate valve handy, so you can turn the water to your house back on sooner.

2. Cut off the water to your home.

3. Cut in the tee.

4. Install a short piece of pipe in the tee outlet and install a gate valve.

5. Close the gate valve and turn the water to your house back on. If you've done your work well, there will be no leaks.

6. Once you have the gate valve in place, proceed from the valve to your irrigation feed. If you prefer to work from the irrigation pipe to the valve you can, but I've always preferred to start at the valve.

HAVING THE RIGHT CONNECTIONS

running water pipes for an upstairs bathroom. When he tied the riser pipes for the bathroom into the pipes in the basement, he mistook one of the heat pipes for a potable hot-water pipe. The result was anything but desirable. Imagine turning on your shower and having dirty boiler water spray down on you. If a professional plumber can make such a mistake, you can imagine how easy it might be for an average homeowner to get confused about which pipe is which.

Mistaking Brass Pipe for Copper

Brass pipe can look like copper pipe. There isn't a lot of brass pipe still in use, but there is enough to make it worth mentioning. I hate to admit it, but I actually mistook brass pipe for copper pipe on one occasion. My only excuse is that the place where I made the mistake was very dark, and it didn't take me long to realize what was going on. Even so, if I can confuse brass pipe with copper pipe, with all my years in the trade, you could certainly make the same mistake.

If you suspect that you're working with brass pipe, trace the pipe to a fitting and see if the joint is made with a threaded connection or a soldered connection. Brass pipe can be cut with standard copper cutters. The pipe will cut harder than copper, but you might not notice the difference. You will, however, know that you are not working with copper as soon as you try to put a fitting on the end of the pipe — it won't go on.

Should you run up against brass pipe, you must remove a section of the pipe so that female threads are available to you at two ends. Then you can use male adapters and the pipe of your choice to span the distance between the brass fittings.

Cutting into a Pipe with Bad Valves

Bad valves can result in bad experiences. When you close the cut-off valve to the pipe into which you will be cutting, make sure the valve is working by closing the valve and opening your faucets to see if all the water pressure has been cut off. I've seen several plumbers fail to take this step and wind up in a wet scene. Old valves don't always work, especially if they rely on washers for a dependable seal. The last thing you want to do is to cut into a pipe that you think is turned off, but is, in reality, stoked with full water pressure.

If you have a valve that is not working, you may be able to cut your water off at your water meter. If your meter is outside, you will probably need a water key to reach the cut-off. If you are baffled, call your local public works office and ask them to cut your water off, assuming that you get your water from a city main. If you are on a well, all you have to do is cut off the electrical power to the pump. In this case, it will take a few minutes for all of the existing pressure to drain out of your pressure tank, but if the power to the pump is off, the water will stop soon.

Dirt In Your Pipes

It is not uncommon to get dirt in your pipes when working with underground piping. This usually isn't much of a problem, but if you don't flush the pipes before you connect your irrigation gear, the dirt may plug up filters and cause all kinds of trouble. Always flush your pipes before you connect your sprinklers or other irrigation gear.

Making the Irrigation System Operational

ONCE YOU'VE INSTALLED YOUR irrigation system, putting it into operation will not take long. There may be some minor bugs to work out of your system, but most problems you may encounter, if any, will not be major.

First-Time Start-Up Procedures

Once your system is installed, rushing to turn on valves can create problems. Failure to follow proper procedures can result in damaged equipment, flash floods in your home, and similar unwanted experiences. What is the right way to turn on your system? There is a recommended step-by-step procedure that varies a bit depending on the type of irrigation system installed.

If you are using a simple system, such as a garden hose and sprinkler, there are no elaborate procedures to follow. The most that could go wrong is a missing or malfunctioning hose washer (the round washer in the female hose connectors used with hose bibbs and sprinklers). If the washer is bad, just replace it, which doesn't require tools and is easy to do.

As you move up to more sophisticated systems, the start-up requirements become a little more complex. Don't let this alarm you — all aspects of the start-up are well within your skill level if you have installed your own system.

Mobile Irrigation Systems

Mobile irrigation systems include a simple hose sprinkler and garden hose, a system where the irrigation equipment is mounted on wheels and the irrigation hose is coiled around a reel, and larger systems with irrigation heads mounted on tripods, staked into the ground, or set out on legs.

These systems are easy to bring up to speed. The connection between the hose/pipe and the irrigation head is usually a simple one. The other end of the hose/pipe connects to a water service. Getting this type of system into operation simply involves securing the connections at both ends and turning on the water.

Overhead Systems

Overhead irrigation systems can be a bit more complicated to make operational on-line because there's more to go wrong. For example, there are probably several valves, and there may be a quantity of sprinkler heads. The more parts to a system, the greater the likelihood that you may run into problems.

There may be debris in your pipes that can foul filters and clog sprinklers. If your new irrigation system is equipped with filters and sprinkler heads, remove these devices prior to turning on the water. When you first turn on the water to your irrigation system, flush the system completely with the filters and sprinkler heads removed. In the case of overhead

systems with perforated pipe, it will not be necessary to remove filters or heads since there are none.

There probably are at least a few valves incorporated into your overhead system. You may not have any problem with them, but it is not uncommon for valves to develop small leaks around the packing nuts surrounding the valve stems. If water is bubbling out around a packing nut, a turn or two of the nut with a wrench should stop the flow. Once you're sure there are no leaks in your overhead system, you can turn it on.

Underground Systems

Underground systems are the most complicated of all standard residential irrigation systems. Often there are several valves involved with an underground system, and some of them are controlled electrically. The control panel alone can present more than just a few problems. Before starting up, decide which nozzle to use. Many systems offer a half-dozen or more nozzles for various watering situations. After selecting the best one for your job, you must learn to aim it properly at the desired site, which can take a little practice.

Nozzles

Quality sprinkler heads can be fitted to a wide selection of nozzles, allowing versatility in your watering patterns. You may find that the sprinklers you've installed are not equipped with the nozzles you want. Each system has its own procedure for installing nozzles; refer to the paperwork that comes with your sprinkler heads for specific instructions. Following are instructions for replacing nozzles on several popular sprinkler models.

One sprinkler brand requires no tool for changing nozzles. You simply pull up the riser of the sprinkler by grasping the head, unscrew the existing nozzle, and screw in the replacement. The manufacturer advises that the raised dot found on top of the head be aligned with the right edge of the spray arc. (The right edge as established by standing behind the sprinkler's spray pattern.) The manufacturer also advises to flush out the system first by removing the internal assemblies on each lateral line for the last sprinkler head. The internal assemblies can then be replaced and the arc and radius for each head set.

Another popular type of sprinkler head design requires a special hex-end tool for nozzle installation. The tool is placed into the nozzle opening and pressed downward, forcing the nozzle up and out. A new nozzle is then placed on the riser, and pushed down and in so that a barbed retainer on the underside of the nozzle engages to hold it in place. A small tab is then folded over and snapped into place on top of the sprinkler nozzle. To replace this type of nozzle, the hex-end wrench is used to pry up the identifier tab, which can then be grasped and pulled up and out at a 45-degree angle.

Other sprinkler head models use retainer screws to hold the nozzles in place. For some types, nozzles are removed by loosening the retainers and turning the water on to blow the nozzles out of their risers. For others, needle-nose pliers are required to remove the nozzles. There are many ways to change nozzles, so follow the instructions that come with your equipment.

Turf Cups

It is possible to buy sprinklers equipped with turf cups, which allow the sprinkler to be concealed with grass. The cup, made of rubber, makes the sprinkler system practically invisible. There are, however, a few tips for installing turf cups.

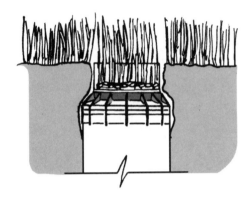

A rubber turf cup disguises the top of your retractable sprinkler head. Turf is inserted in the cup to blend with the surrounding grass.

The top edge of a turf cup should not be installed higher than the finished grade level of the ground in which its riser is buried. It is recommended that turf cups be installed in grassy areas where reel mowers are used. Once the cup is in place, fill it with an established turf section. It is best to use turf consisting of grass identical to the grass where the sprinkler is located. Don't attempt to use grass seed in the cup, as the seeds will be washed away when the sprinkler head cycles up and down. According to one manufacturer of a turf cup, you should tend to the new turf (in the cup) for a period of at least two weeks. The

MAKING THE IRRIGATION SYSTEM OPERATIONAL

company recommends pressing the turf plug into the cup daily for this period of time to establish a root system.

Arc and Radius Adjustments

Arc and radius adjustments, like nozzle replacement, vary from system to system. Refer to the instructions provided with your equipment for exact details on how to adjust the arc and radius of your sprinklers. However, I can tell you how this job is done with two types of sprinklers.

With one residential sprinkler head, a special wrench (available from the sprinkler manufacturer) and a screwdriver are needed to adjust the arc and radius. The first step is to lift the riser and to rachet it into alignment so that the arc designator is lined up with the right-hand border of the coverage area. Next, the special wrench, or a screwdriver, is used to turn an adjustment screw counterclockwise, which increases the arc and the discharge rate. The radius is adjusted by holding the arc stationary with the wrench while turning the adjustment screw with a screwdriver.

Another type of sprinkler requires that the nozzle turret be turned to the left stop and then to the right stop, which is also the fixed side of the arc, where it is held while all adjustments are made. A special wrench is also needed to work with this particular type of sprinkler. To increase the arc, the wrench is inserted into an adjustment socket located on top of the sprinkler and turned clockwise. To decrease the arc, the wrench is turned counterclockwise. Radius adjustment with this type of sprinkler is done by changing nozzles.

Controllers

Controllers can be a bit complicated to set. If you have trouble setting the clock on your VCR, plan to spend some quality time with your controller. Like the other system components discussed, controllers vary substantially. Follow the manufacturer's instructions. While I can't give you specific information about the settings on your controller, I can give you a brief rundown on the types of settings you may have to make in order to get your system up and running.

All controllers have a clock and calendar to set. There are usually options for setting automatic watering, semi-automatic watering, manual watering, or watering with a remote sensor, an accessory that measures recent rainfall and controls the irrigation system accordingly.

Most owner's manuals for controllers are written for the average person to understand. I recommend that you read your manual from cover to cover before making any adjustments or settings. This first reading will familiarize you with your controller.

Monitoring Your System

To ensure desired irrigation results, you must monitor your system. When you first put it into operation, check the water's arc and radius. Confirm that you are receiving uniform coverage with no wet or dry spots. With a stationary irrigation system, this type of inspection should only be needed once or twice. Mobile systems require more frequent monitoring, since they are never set up in exactly the same way twice.

If you find it necessary to make minor adjustments while monitoring the actions of your irrigation equipment, refer to the manufacturer's instructions. If you cannot find that information, my advice is to call the manufacturer. If you purchased a quality system, support staff will be available to help. Some irrigation equipment is sensitive, and none of it should be dealt with in a reckless manner. If you do not know what to do or how to do it, my advice is to ask for professional help.

Suggested Reading

Binetti, Marianne. *Tips for Carefree Landscapes.* Pownal, VT: Garden Way Publishing,1990.

Campbell, Stu. *The Home Water Supply: How to Find, Filter, Store, and Conserve It.* Garden Way Publishing, 1983.

Editors of Garden Way Publishing. *Just the Facts! Dozens of Garden Charts, Thousands of Gardening Answers.* Pownal, VT: Garden Way Publishing, 1993.

Editors of Garden Way Publishing. *The Big Book of Gardening Skills.* Pownal, VT: Garden Way Publishing, 1993.

Franklin, Stuart. *Building a Healthy Lawn.* Pownal, VT: Garden Way Publishing, 1988.

Glattstein, Judy. *Waterscaping: Plants and Ideas for Natural and Created Water Gardens.* Pownal, VT: Garden Way Publishing, 1994.

Kourik, Robert. *Gray Water: Use In the Landscape.* Santa Rosa, CA: Metamorphic Press, 1988.

Hart, Rhonda Massingham. *Dirt-Cheap Gardening: Hundreds of Ways to Save Money in Your Garden.* Pownal, VT: Garden Way Publishing, 1995.

Lawrence, Mike, editor. *Step-by-Step Outdoor Stonework: Over twenty easy-to-build projects for your patio and garden.* Pownal, VT: Storey Publishing, 1995.

O'Keefe, John M. *Water-Conserving Gardens and Landscapes.* Pownal, VT: Storey Publishing, 1992.

Raymond, Dick. *Down-to-Earth Natural Lawn Care.* Pownal, VT: Storey Publishing, 1993.

Whitner, Jan Kowalczewski. *Stonescaping: A Guide to Using Stone in Your Garden.* Pownal, VT: Garden Way Publishing, 1992.

~ Index ~

Page references in *italic* indicate illustrations; those in **bold** indicate tables.